Cambridge
Global English

WORKBOOK 12

Ingrid Wisniewska & Susan Hutchison

CAMBRIDGE
UNIVERSITY PRESS

Shaftesbury Road, Cambridge CB2 8EA, United Kingdom

One Liberty Plaza, 20th Floor, New York, NY 10006, USA

477 Williamstown Road, Port Melbourne, VIC 3207, Australia

314–321, 3rd Floor, Plot 3, Splendor Forum, Jasola District Centre, New Delhi – 110025, India

103 Penang Road, #05–06/07, Visioncrest Commercial, Singapore 238467

Cambridge University Press is part of the University of Cambridge.

It furthers the University's mission by disseminating knowledge in the pursuit of education, learning and research at the highest international levels of excellence.

www.cambridge.org
Information on this title: www.cambridge.org/9781009398909

© Cambridge University Press & Assessment 2024

This publication is in copyright. Subject to statutory exception and to the provisions of relevant collective licensing agreements, no reproduction of any part may take place without the written permission of Cambridge University Press.

First published 2024

20 19 18 17 16 15 14 13 12 11 10 9 8 7 6 5 4 3 2 1

Printed in Malaysia by Vivar Printing

A catalogue record for this publication is available from the British Library

ISBN 978-1-009-39890-9 Workbook with Digital Access (2 Years)

Additional resources for this publication at www.cambridge.org/go

Cambridge University Press has no responsibility for the persistence or accuracy of URLs for external or third-party internet websites referred to in this publication, and does not guarantee that any content on such websites is, or will remain, accurate or appropriate. Information regarding prices, travel timetables, and other factual information given in this work is correct at the time of first printing but Cambridge University Press does not guarantee the accuracy of such information thereafter.

This text has not been through the Cambridge International endorsement process.

NOTICE TO TEACHERS IN THE UK
It is illegal to reproduce any part of this work in material form (including photocopying and electronic storage) except under the following circumstances:
(i) where you are abiding by a licence granted to your school or institution by the Copyright Licensing Agency;
(ii) where no such licence exists, or where you wish to exceed the terms of a licence, and you have gained the written permission of Cambridge University Press;
(iii) where you are allowed to reproduce without permission under the provisions of Chapter 3 of the Copyright, Designs and Patents Act 1988, which covers, for example, the reproduction of short passages within certain types of educational anthology and reproduction for the purposes of setting examination questions.

2023 CAMBRIDGE DEDICATED TEACHER AWARDS

Teachers play an important part in shaping futures. Our Dedicated Teacher Awards recognise the hard work that teachers put in every day.

Thank you to everyone who nominated this year; we have been inspired and moved by all of your stories. Well done to all of our nominees for your dedication to learning and for inspiring the next generation of thinkers, leaders and innovators.

CONGRATULATIONS TO OUR INCREDIBLE WINNERS!

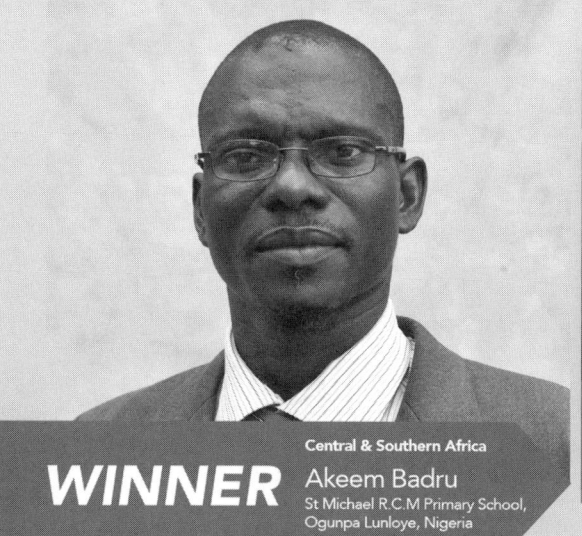

WINNER — Central & Southern Africa
Akeem Badru
St Michael R.C.M Primary School, Ogunpa Lunloye, Nigeria

Regional Winner: East & South Asia
Gaurav Sharma
FirstSteps School, India

Regional Winner: North & South America
Nathalie Roy
Glasgow Middle School, United States

Regional Winner: Australia, New Zealand & South-East Asia
Goh Kok Ming
SJKC Hua Lian 1, Malaysia

Regional Winner: Middle East & North Africa
Uzma Siraj
Future World School, Pakistan

Regional Winner: Europe
Selçuk Yusuf Arslan
Atatürk MTAL, Turkey

For more information about our dedicated teachers and their stories, go to **dedicatedteacher.cambridge.org**

CAMBRIDGE UNIVERSITY PRESS

Brighter Thinking
Better Learning

Contents

	How to use this book	6
1	**Relationships and role models**	**8**
	Think about it: 21st-century families	8
	Sociology: Someone to look up to	10
	Use of English: Attitudinal adverbs	12
	Use of English: *that* clauses	14
	Academic writing: A discussion essay	16
	Check your progress	18
2	**Problem or opportunity?**	**20**
	Think about it: Developing a growth mindset	20
	Psychology: The benefits of play	22
	Use of English: Modals for probability and possibility	24
	Use of English: Parts of speech	26
	Academic writing: Describing data in charts and graphs	28
	Check your progress	30
3	**Then and now**	**32**
	Think about it: The impact of artificial light on insects	32
	Medicine and biology: The effects of stress	34
	Use of English: *Not only… but also…* and *Neither… nor*	36
	Use of English: Formal conditional structures	38
	Academic writing: A proposal	40
	Check your progress	42
4	**Visual arts**	**44**
	Think about it: Looking at arts and crafts	44
	Art: Visual literacy as a life skill	46
	Use of English: Adjectives modified with extreme adverbs	48
	Use of English: Impersonal passive reporting verbs	50
	Academic writing: An argument essay	52
	Check your progress	54
5	**The benefits and risks of artificial intelligence (AI)**	**56**
	Think about it: The role of AI in customer service	56
	Computer science: Human–robot interaction	58
	Use of English: Rhetorical questions	60
	Use of English: Subordinating conjunctions	62
	Academic writing: An agree/disagree essay	64
	Check your progress	66

6 What it is to be human — 68

- Think about it: The secrets of a long and healthy life — 68
- History and economics: An edible history — 70
- Use of English: Modal verbs for speculating and making deductions — 72
- Use of English: Passive voice — 74
- Academic writing: Summarising — 76
- Check your progress — 78

7 Tiny wonders — 80

- Think about it: The magic of microscopic marine organisms — 80
- Biology: Tiny creatures — 82
- Use of English: Prefixes in scientific language — 84
- Use of English: Adverbs for report writing — 86
- Academic writing: A report — 88
- Check your progress — 90

8 Sustainability — 92

- Think about it: What is sustainability? — 92
- Business and environmental management: Embracing sustainability — 94
- Use of English: Syntax – premodifying noun phrases — 96
- Use of English: Linking and transition words — 98
- Academic writing: Expository essay — 100
- Check your progress — 102

9 Fabric and fashion — 104

- Think about it: Ancient textiles and clothing — 104
- Cultural studies: The link between culture and fashion — 106
- Use of English: Negative and positive quantifiers — 108
- Use of English: Linking words to show contrast — 110
- Academic writing: Advantages and disadvantages essay — 112
- Check your progress — 114

10 Fiction and the future — 116

- Think about it: Stories from the future — 116
- Literature: Science fiction — 118
- Use of English: *it* and *there* — 120
- Use of English: Hedging language — 122
- Academic writing: Critical analysis – fiction — 124
- Check your progress — 126

Key phrases bank — 128
Irregular verb table — 131
Acknowledgements — 133

CAMBRIDGE GLOBAL ENGLISH 12: WORKBOOK

> How to use this book

This Workbook provides questions for you to practise what you have learnt in class. There is a unit to match each unit in your Coursebook.

Tips to help you with your learning.

WRITING TIP

When answering questions, it is important to support your points by giving examples from your own knowledge and experience.

USE OF ENGLISH

After that first chemistry lesson we quite honestly thought he was a bit silly. But he was just different from all the other teachers. Unfortunately, the rest of them were serious and uninspiring. They'd talk, we'd take notes and that was about it, sadly. It was really boring and obviously it didn't put any of us in the mood for learning. But Mr Gupta would walk into class and make stuff like the periodic table amazingly come alive. He clearly enjoyed what he was doing. I'll always remember what he taught me – well, hopefully I will!

Information to help you find out more about grammar.

Check!

1   Read the journal entry. Underline the adverbs of attitude.

Notice

2   Look at the adverbs of attitude you have underlined.
    Tick the three statements that are true.

    Adverbs of attitude…

    a   express the way something is done ☐
    b   must go at the beginning of a sentence ☐
    c   can go at the beginning, middle or end of a sentence ☐
    d   are used to emphasise someone's feeling about something ☐
    e   may sometimes be preceded by a comma ☐

Use the Cambridge Learner Corpus to get your grammar right!

GET IT RIGHT!

After some verbs, the word *that* can be omitted.

Example:
She told us (that) we couldn't leave class early.

How to use this book

There are opportunities to practise your grammar on the Use of English pages in each unit. Each Use of English lesson is divided into three parts:

Focus: These grammar questions help you to master the basics. →

> **Focus**
> 3 Circle the most appropriate adverb.
>
> a *Fortunately / Sadly*, it was an unusually warm winter so my brother and I couldn't go skiing after all.
>
> b You've got to believe me – I *really / unfortunately* did enjoy the meal your grandmother prepared for us!
>
> c Have you heard the bad news? My best friend Kate's moving overseas with her parents. I'm *obviously / amazingly* going to miss her loads.
>
> d Look at the price tag on those boots – they're so expensive, but *sadly / hopefully* they'll be reduced in the sales soon.

Practice: These grammar questions help you to become more accurate and confident. →

> **Practice**
> 4 In some of these sentences, the attitudinal adverbs are in the wrong place. Rewrite the sentences that are incorrect. Put a tick beside any sentences that are correct.
>
> a If I had to choose, I would buy obviously the cheaper one. ☐
>
> b Our bus was delayed but surprisingly we arrived at the theatre on time. ☐
>
> c Most of our customers are happy clearly with the service. ☐

Challenge: These questions will help you use language fluently and prepare for the next level. →

> **Challenge**
> 5 Fill the gaps with an appropriate adverb.
>
> a He fell during yesterday's match but .... he wasn't injured at all.
>
> b I'd been really looking forward to trying the new restaurant, but .... the food was rather disappointing.
>
> c My brother and I are really close – .... we'll stay that way forever!
>
> d We really enjoy spending time with our grandparents and .... for us, they live quite near us.
>
> e She looks really pale and her hands are shaking. She's .... not feeling very well.

Questions that help you to think about your learning and progress. →

> **REFLECTION**
>
> Write answers to these questions in your notebook.
>
> a Choose five new words from this unit and write a definition for each one in your notebook.
>
> b What did you learn about 'global citizenship' in the unit? Write down some ideas.
>
> c Would you be interested in reading any of the books mentioned in the reading text about role models? If so, which one and why?
>
> d Look back at your discussion essay and find two places where you could provide more information from your own experience to support a point, using 'such as', 'for instance' or 'like'.
>
> e What did you learn about collaborating with others through your work in this unit? What did you do well?

1 Relationships and role models

Think about it: 21st-century families

1 **Read the fact files about two people. Then complete them using words from the box.**

> wouldn't change it for the world   privacy   nuclear family
> interdependent   multigenerational   independent   extended family

Rebecca

I live in a flat with my mum and dad. While this kind of traditional ……………………………….¹ is still quite common in my country, things have started to change in the past few decades. There are all kinds of family arrangements these days. For example, I've got a friend whose grandparents live with him and his parents. I really feel for him – he doesn't have much ……………………………….². My grandmother lives round the corner from us, which is great. I spend a lot of time at her place – she's honestly like a second mother to me. As for my parents and me, I'd say we all get on pretty well together. I feel I can talk to them about anything. I'm an only child so I would say I'm quite ……………………………….³ because I don't have a brother or sister to help me out or do things for me.

1 Relationships and role models

Silas

I live in an ....⁴ with my parents, two younger brothers, my aunt and my grandparents all together in the one house. ....⁵ living is common in my culture, so my family is quite typical. We're a close family and fairly ....⁶ too. For instance, my grandfather helps me with my maths homework and when my aunt has a problem with her laptop, I'll do my best to sort it out. We have a lot of fun together – especially when we're cooking dinner. We're really lucky to have each other. I love my family and I ....⁷.

2   Choose the heading that fits both fact files.

   A   Increasing pressures on family life

   B   Different family shapes and sizes

3   Read the fact files again. Who do these phrases refer to? Circle R for Rebecca, S for Silas or N for neither of them.

   a   appreciates having a secondary parental figure   R   S   N
   b   provides practical support to one particular relative   R   S   N
   c   regrets not having more privacy at home   R   S   N
   d   mentions that family structures have undergone change over time   R   S   N

4   Underline the stressed words in the following sentences from the fact files.

   a   I live in a flat with my mum and dad.
   b   I feel I can talk to them about anything.
   c   I spend a lot of time at her place – she's honestly like a second mum to me.
   d   We have a lot of fun together – especially in the kitchen when we're cooking dinner.

Challenge

5   Write a short text about your family life. Include a heading.

   ....
   ....

> **SPEAKING TIP**
>
> When you want to emphasise what you are saying, you can stress certain words – that is, pronounce them more loudly or slowly, or by pausing briefly after you say them. We usually stress content words in a sentence, rather than function words (*about, and, the, to, it*, etc.).
>
> I **love** my **family** and I **wouldn't** change it for the **world**.

Sociology: Someone to look up to

1 Skim the four extracts and match them with the type of text.

book summary ☐
dictionary entry ☐
teen blog ☐
research article ☐

a **anti-role model:** a person who displays **undesirable** characteristics and **antisocial behaviour** that you want to avoid as you plan your life and make progress towards your personal goals.

b Abstract

Background

Identity formation is a dynamic process that begins in adolescence. During this time, children look to adults as **role models**.

Objective

The aim of this research is to see if there is a relationship between identified role models, and adolescents' interest in education, confidence, happiness and physical activity.

c Bursting with fun facts and illustrations, it charts the lives and achievements of some of the most inspiring and **controversial** women in history. Among those featured are painter Frida Kahlo, nurse Mary Seacole and civil rights activist Rosa Parks.

d I really admire Dylan Conrique. I love her singing and she has an amazing voice. She seems like a kind, amazing human and everything she does is awesome!
– Taylor, 13

2 Match the words in bold in the extracts with the definitions below.

a not wanted or approved of ....

b people with qualities that others admire and try to copy ....

c a way of behaving that is harmful or annoying to other people or society

....

d causing a lot of angry public discussion and disagreement ....

e a person who displays negative qualities that we hope to avoid in our

own lives ....

1 Relationships and role models

3 Read the article, then answer the questions.

> Role models have a clear effect on how children express their originality as they are growing up. To encourage inventiveness and creativity in their children, parents should allow them to look for their own role models. For a start, there are many good role models to be found in real stories of amazing people throughout history. Human rights campaigner Malala Yousafzai, for example, was inspired by a woman called Meena – a human rights activist in Afghanistan.
>
> In some cases, however, fiction may provide even better role models, partly because fictional characters can achieve things that have never been done before. The people who invented the submarine and helicopter were fascinated by Jules Verne's descriptions in his novels *Twenty Thousand Leagues Under the Sea* and *The Clipper of the Clouds*. Throughout *The Clipper of the Clouds*, which features a fictional flying machine called the *Albatross*, Verne explores the nature of flight and its effects on humanity. As young people discover creative and ingenious ideas in history and fiction, the fear of consequences disappears. They no longer concern themselves with what might happen if they don't succeed.
>
> Perhaps it won't be too long before the next generation of inventors and influencers starts looking to more recent stories and films for inspiration. The *Harry Potter* series, for example, is bursting with original thoughts and ideas.

a   Who served as a positive role model for Malala Yousafzai?

    ....

b   Which **two** inventions may have been inspired by works of fiction?

    ....

c   Which works of fiction may inspire young people to develop creativity and originality in future?

    ....

4 Read the article again. Circle true (T), false (F) or not given (NG) for each of the following statements.

a   The text is taken from a book summary.   T   F   NG

b   The writer of the text is a parent.   T   F   NG

c   Characters in novels may sometimes inspire young people
    more than real-life role models.   T   F   NG

d   The underlined phrase in paragraph 2 means 'they become
    less willing to take risks'.   T   F   NG

Challenge

5 In your notebook, write 150 words about a fictional character or a person in real life who you look up to.

Use of English: Attitudinal adverbs

USE OF ENGLISH

After that first chemistry lesson we quite honestly thought he was a bit silly. But he was just different from all the other teachers. Unfortunately, the rest of them were serious and uninspiring. They'd talk, we'd take notes and that was about it, sadly. It was really boring and obviously it didn't put any of us in the mood for learning. But Mr Gupta would walk into class and make stuff like the periodic table amazingly come alive. He clearly enjoyed what he was doing. I'll always remember what he taught me – well, hopefully I will!

Check!

1 Read the journal entry. Underline the adverbs of attitude.

Notice

2 Look at the adverbs of attitude you have underlined. Tick the three statements that are true.

Adverbs of attitude...

a express the way something is done ☐

b must go at the beginning of a sentence ☐

c can go at the beginning, middle or end of a sentence ☐

d are used to emphasise someone's feeling about something ☐

e may sometimes be preceded by a comma ☐

Focus

3 **Circle the most appropriate adverb.**

a *Fortunately / Sadly*, it was an unusually warm winter so my brother and I couldn't go skiing after all.

b You've got to believe me – I *really / unfortunately* did enjoy the meal your grandmother prepared for us!

c Have you heard the bad news? My best friend Kate's moving overseas with her parents. I'm *obviously / amazingly* going to miss her loads.

d Look at the price tag on those boots – they're so expensive, but *sadly / hopefully* they'll be reduced in the sales soon.

GET IT RIGHT!

Remember to put the adverb in the correct position in the sentence – it needs to go before the verb.

Example:
*This summer I can **hopefully go** and visit my cousins.* (not *go hopefully*)

Practice

4 In some of these sentences, the attitudinal adverbs are in the wrong place. Rewrite the sentences that are incorrect. Put a tick beside any sentences that are correct.

a If I had to choose, I would buy obviously the cheaper one.

....

b Our bus was delayed but surprisingly we arrived at the theatre on time.

....

c Most of our customers are happy clearly with the service.

....

d I have a big family and we all luckily get on very well.

....

Challenge

5 Fill the gaps with an appropriate adverb.

a He fell during yesterday's match but .... he wasn't injured at all.

b I'd been really looking forward to trying the new restaurant, but .... the food was rather disappointing.

c My brother and I are really close – .... we'll stay that way forever!

d We really enjoy spending time with our grandparents and .... for us, they live quite near us.

e She looks really pale and her hands are shaking. She's .... not feeling very well.

Use of English: *that* clauses

USE OF ENGLISH

One mystery that has confused scientists for a long time is 'yawn contagion'[1]. This refers to the urge we have to yawn when we see other people do it.

Although some researchers first thought that this urge was a kind of social empathy, which enables people to connect with each other[2], it remained unclear whether we 'catch' a yawn or not.

However, a recent study by Professor Elisabetta Palagi at the University of Pisa in Italy has shown that the[3] most important factor is the relationship between the yawner and the person that hears or sees it, rather than the nationality, sex or age of the people involved.

The research team studied cases of yawning among a group of adults from around the world over the course of one year. **The results showed that people are most likely to catch or pass on a yawn when interacting with family members**[4], followed on a decreasing scale by friends, then acquaintances and finally strangers. **Children develop contagious yawning at the age of four or five – around the same time that they begin to understand the emotions of other people.**[5]

Check!

1 Read the information about yawning.
  Match the bold phrases with the uses of *that* below.

  a Define: to provide additional information about the head noun or phrase. [1] [ ]

  b Evaluate: to signpost a person's viewpoint. [ ]

  c Compare: to compare two ideas. [ ] [ ]

Notice

2 Read the information again. Circle true (T) or false (F) for each of these statements about the use of *that* clauses.

  a *Who* or *which* can never be used instead of *that*.   T   F

  b *That* can be omitted after some verbs.   T   F

  c *That* is never preceded by a comma.   T   F

Focus

3 Match the beginnings (a–e) and the endings (i–v) to make correct sentences.

a Yawn contagion is a phenomenon that

b The researchers considered a number of different factors that

c The research team discovered that

d It was a study that

e Professor Elisabetta Palagi is one of the researchers that

i people are less likely to respond to a yawn with another yawn if the other person is a stranger.

ii sampled people from many different countries.

iii has been a puzzle for many years.

iv were associated with contagious yawns, such as gender and age.

v helped write the study.

Practice

4 Which two sentences are missing the word *that*? Mark where in the sentence *that* should go.

a Why didn't you mention you were planning a skiing trip? I would have come!

b I explained I would be late for the meeting this morning.

c Empathy is a word describes the ability to understand the feelings of another person.

d Do you know anyone took part in the research study?

GET IT RIGHT!
After some verbs, the word *that* can be omitted.

Example:
She told us (that) we couldn't leave class early.

Challenge

5 Complete these sentences using a *that* clause.

a Students generally like lessons

   that are fun and motivating.

b I didn't manage to finish all the homework

   ....

c Have you finished the book

   ....

d I like the kind of film

   ....

e A good friend is someone

   ....

CAMBRIDGE GLOBAL ENGLISH 12: WORKBOOK

Academic writing: A discussion essay

1 Look at the two pictures. Make notes on the following questions in your notebook.

- What might the families enjoy about spending time together in these different ways?
- What do you think they may be talking about in each situation?

2 Read the essay question and the sample introduction and conclusion. What should you do in a discussion essay?

A include language from the essay question ☐

B state your own opinion at the beginning and at the end ☐

Some people say that sitting down and eating a meal together is the best way for families to enjoy quality time together. Others say that families can enjoy quality time equally well in other ways. Discuss both views and give your own opinion.

Introduction
There are many ways in which families can appreciate spending time in each other's company. While some people take the view that strong family bonds can be formed equally well away from the dinner table, I firmly believe that parents and children who regularly sit round a table to enjoy a plate of food connect with each other.

Conclusion
To sum up, I think that shared mealtimes are the best way for families to connect with each other on a regular basis. What could be better than enjoying a plate of food and some good conversation?

3 Which view does the student agree with in the question – the first view or the second view?

....

> **WRITING TIP**
>
> When answering questions, it is important to support your points by giving examples from your own knowledge and experience.

16

1 Relationships and role models

4 Read the following points a student has made about family meals.
Complete the sentences with your own ideas, using words and phrases from the box.

| for instance   like   such as   for example |

a   <u>I really believe that</u> parents and children can spend quality time together away from the dinner table. This could involve spending time outdoors as a family ....

b   <u>It is important to remember that</u> family meals enable children to learn important life skills ....

c   <u>Some people think that</u> in today's fast-paced society, it can be difficult for parents and children to find the time to sit down and enjoy meals together at home ....

d   <u>There is no doubt that</u> mealtimes provide an ideal chance for families to ....

5 Look at the underlined phrases in Exercise 4.
Which phrase can be used to introduce views of people you don't agree with?

6 Complete the graphic organiser with your own ideas about the topic.

| Eating a meal | Best way for families to spend quality time together | Other ways |

7 Write your own essay in your notebook. Then complete the checklist.

Have you…

☐ rephrased the words in the essay question?
☐ stated your opinion in the introduction and the conclusion?
☐ used appropriate phrases such as 'I firmly believe' to express your views?
☐ considered both views?
☐ supported your points with relevant examples?

Check your progress

Vocabulary

1 **Circle the correct answers.**

    a   It's just me and my two children at home. We're a/an ……… family.

          A nuclear

          B multi-generational

          C extended

    b   A person who exhibits the opposite behaviour and qualities to those you want to follow yourself can be described as a/an ………

          A role model

          B anti-role model

          C global citizen

    c   Yawns are least contagious when they come from ………

          A family

          B acquaintances

          C strangers

    d   The delay in which a yawn is passed on is closely linked to the ……… between the people involved.

          A nationalities

          B relationships

          C ages

    e   One ……… of having a role model is that they can inspire you to achieve your personal goals.

          A drawback

          B disadvantage

          C benefit

Grammar

2 **Circle two words from each set that could correctly complete the text.**

Moving to a foreign country can be a life-changing experience. It can completely alter your outlook on life, enabling you to meet new people, become familiar with a different culture and perhaps even learn another language. However, before setting out on your new adventure, you *obviously / surprisingly / clearly*[1] need to make some important decisions. One of these is choosing where to live. For me, opting to live with a host family was *hopefully / honestly / luckily*[2] the best choice I could have made. I felt a bit apprehensive when I first arrived, but *fortunately / hopefully / luckily*[3] those feelings didn't last long because the family was so warm and welcoming. We'd all sit round the table and eat together and go on trips to the beach. They *honestly / surprisingly / unfortunately*[4] made me feel like part of the family. I spent a whole year with them but the time went *amazingly / surprisingly / clearly*[5] quickly. It's an experience I'll *obviously / sadly / hopefully*[6] never forget!

1 Relationships and role models

Reading

3 **Skim the information below and decide who the intended audience is.**

- A university researchers
- B politicians
- C parents and educators

> A survey of 13- and 14-year-olds carried out by academics at Cardiff University showed that those who argue 'a lot', compared to those who 'never' argued, were more likely to have been involved with a human rights organisation in the past 12 months and to have contacted a politician or signed a petition.
>
> Professor Sally Power, who led the study, said: 'Traditionally, rows between teenagers have been seen as an unwelcome and stressful part of growing up. In actual fact, our research indicates arguments may be one route through which young people acquire skills of debate that enable them to have higher levels of civic engagement.'

4 **Which statement best sums up the ideas in the text in Exercise 3?**

- A Young people are increasingly having arguments with others about political issues.
- B Young people who frequently have disagreements tend to be more interested in community issues.

Speaking

5 **Use phrases from the box to write your responses to questions a–c in your notebook.**

> I firmly believe that
> There is no doubt that
> It's impossible to argue with the fact that
> It's important to remember that

- a Do you think that children should be taught debating skills at school? Why or why not?
- b What kind of topics would be interesting for teenagers to have debates about? Why?
- c How important are role models in our lives? In your opinion, what makes a good role model?

Writing

6 **Read the essay question and underline the key words.**

Some people say that it is better to have a few close friends. Others say that a large group of friends is preferable. Discuss both these views and give your own opinion.

7 **Write an introduction to the essay by paraphrasing the question and stating your opinion and main reason.**

REFLECTION

Write answers to these questions in your notebook.

- a Choose five new words from this unit and write a definition for each one in your notebook.
- b What did you learn about 'global citizenship' in the unit? Write down some ideas.
- c Would you be interested in reading any of the books mentioned in the reading text about role models? If so, which one and why?
- d Look back at your discussion essay and find two places where you could provide more information from your own experience to support a point, using 'such as', 'for instance' or 'like'.
- e What did you learn about collaborating with others through your work in this unit? What did you do well?

2 Problem or opportunity?

Think about it: Developing a growth mindset

1. **Draw lines to match the areas of work (a–e) with the jobs (i–v).**

   a   aviation   i   athlete

   b   hospitality   ii   surgeon

   c   healthcare   iii   pilot

   d   sport   iv   inventor

   e   design/technology   v   chef

2. **Which of the jobs in Exercise 1 might the following statements apply to? Give reasons for your choices.**

   a   It is particularly important to avoid making mistakes.

   ....

   b   It helps if you are willing to take risks.

   ....

   c   It is important to view mistakes in a positive way and learn from them.

   ....

   d   It is advisable never to admit to failure.

   ....

   e   It is a good idea to ask questions if you're unsure about something.

   ....

2 Problem or opportunity?

3 Look back at the statements in Exercise 2.
Which are characteristics of a growth mindset and which of a fixed mindset?

Growth mindset ☐ ☐ ☐   Fixed mindset ☐ ☐

4 Skim the text. Which two areas of work in Exercise 1 are mentioned?

Our children can only truly succeed if they first learn how to fail. Consider that world-class figure skaters fall over more often during practice than low-level figure skaters. This seems **contradictory**. Why are the really good skaters falling over the most?

The reason is actually quite simple. Top skaters are constantly challenging themselves, attempting jumps that stretch their limitations. This is why they fall over so often, but is precisely why they learn so fast. Shizuka Arakawa of Japan estimates that she endured some 20 000 falls as she progressed from beginner to an Olympic champion.

Lower-level skaters have a quite different approach. They attempt jumps they can already do, remaining within their **comfort zone**. This is why they don't fall over. In a superficial sense, they look successful, because they are always on their feet. But by never failing, they never progress.

What is true of skating is also true of life. James Dyson worked through 5126 failed prototypes for his dual cyclone vacuum cleaner before coming up with the design that made his fortune. These **setbacks** were essential to the pathway of learning. As Dyson put it: 'You can't develop new technology unless you test new ideas and learn when things go wrong. Failure is essential to invention.'

In a complex world, messing up is inevitable. It is those individuals and institutions that have the resilience and flexibility to face up to **imperfection** and failure, learn the lessons and adapt, which ultimately **excel**.

5 Choose the best title for the text.

A If at first you don't succeed, try, try again!

B Avoid failure at all costs if you want to get ahead!

6 Write the bold words in the article next to the correct the meanings.

a referring to situations where you are not challenged ....

b to be very good at something ....

c a fault or weakness ....

d showing that the opposite is true ....

e things that delay or stop a process from developing ....

Challenge

7 Write full answers to the following questions in your notebook.

a When was the last time you overcame a personal challenge?

b Do you agree with Dyson's view that 'failure is essential to invention'? Why or why not?

Psychology: The benefits of play

> **READING TIP**
>
> Remember that the title and lead-in to a text can help you make predictions about its content.

1 Read the title and the first sentence of the article. How might children benefit from playing with dolls? Write down some ideas in your notebook.

2 Skim the first paragraph of the text. Underline the sentence that describes the benefits. Did the writer include any of your ideas?

The benefits of playing with dolls

Playing with dolls encourages children to talk more about others' thoughts and emotions.

Research suggests that playing imaginary games with dolls could help children develop social skills, theory of mind and **empathy**. Dr Sarah Gerson, the neuroscientist who led the work, said that the educational value of playing with Lego and construction toys was widely accepted, but the benefits of playing with dolls sometimes appeared to have been **overlooked**.

The study involved 33 boys and girls aged between four and eight, who were given some dolls and accessories such as an ambulance or a horse to play with.

They were left to play **spontaneously**, but their speech was monitored and they were also fitted with a specialised cap containing a form of brain-imaging technology which makes it possible to track brain activity while the subject is freely moving around.

The study found that the children talked more about others' thoughts and emotions, a **concept** known as internal state language, when playing with dolls, compared with playing creative games on a computer tablet.

They were also more likely to address the dolls in the second person, talking to them directly, whereas the characters on the computer screen they tended to refer to in the third person. No difference was observed between boys and girls.

Children typically start to show signs of internal state language around the age of four. At this age, they begin to voice their thoughts aloud, indicating that they are considering the thoughts, feelings and desires of themselves and others.

'These skills are really important for interacting with other people, learning from other people, and **navigating** a variety of social situations,' Gerson said.

3 Read the text again. Are the following statements true (T), false (F) or not given (NG)?

a There is broad agreement among researchers about the benefits of playing building games. T F NG

b The participants in the study were given male and female dolls to play with. T F NG

c Brain-imaging technology was used to monitor the children's verbal communication during play. T F NG

d The research revealed that boys and girls addressed their dolls differently. T F NG

e Children generally develop empathy prior to the age of four. T F NG

4 Write the words in bold from the article next to the correct meaning.

a failed to see or notice something ....

b the ability to understand another person's feelings ....

c finding the right way to deal with a situation ....

d done naturally, without being forced or practised ....

e an idea or a principle that is connected with something abstract ....

Use of English: Modals for probability and possibility

USE OF ENGLISH

Check!

1 Underline the words or phrases in the sentences that relate to possibility.

   Example: I <u>might</u> be home late tonight – I have a meeting after work.

   a The temperature in the mountains can fall below freezing point at this time of year.

   b The phone's ringing. It could be Jack.

   c I've done no preparation for the interview, so I'm hardly likely to get the job.

   d I've checked the weather forecast – it's highly probable that it will snow this weekend.

   e That can't possibly be Sunita at the door – she flew to America yesterday.

Notice

2 Write the correct letters (a–e) in the boxes.

   Which sentence in Exercise 1 talks about:

   a a feeling of certainty about something happening in future?

   b a more general possibility of something happening?

   c a belief that something is impossible based on evidence/knowledge?

   d a very small chance of something happening in future?

   e possibility in the present or the future?

Focus

3 **Circle the correct option to complete the sentences.**

   a She has never tried that jump before so it's *highly probable / hardly likely* she'll be successful on her first attempt.

   b It *might / can* get really cold in the mountains even in autumn.

   c I think that this hockey competition *can / might* be really challenging for him.

   d My daughter has lost her favourite toy. I've looked all over the house. I haven't looked in the garden though, so it *can't / may* be there.

   e The pitch is soaking from all the rain so it's *highly probable / hardly likely* that tomorrow's match will be cancelled.

Practice

4 Some of these sentences use the modal verb *can* incorrectly. Correct the sentences. Tick the sentences that are already correct.

a I'm not sure why she's late. She can be stuck in heavy traffic.

....

b It's a really good restaurant so it can often be crowded at weekends.

....

c You can't possibly be tired – you've been sleeping all day!

....

d James looks rather pale. I think he can be unwell.

....

e He speaks very quietly so it can be difficult to understand him at times.

....

f There can be a lot of people at the concert tonight.

....

> **GET IT RIGHT!**
>
> Remember, it is not possible to use *can* when speculating about present or past situations.
>
> Example:
> *I've not seen her for a few days – she **could/might/may** be on holiday.*
> (not *can be*)

5 Complete these sentences using the correct form of a modal verb from the box. Sometimes more than one modal verb may be possible.

can   could   may   might

a If you want to win this match, you .... afford to make any mistakes.

b I think we should call off tomorrow's match, but other people .... agree with me.

c It .... be really difficult to find a parking space in the city centre at weekends.

d You'd better bring an umbrella because it .... rain later.

Challenge

6 Answer these questions using words and phrases of probability or possibility.

a What is one thing you might do next year?

....

....

b What do you think you're hardly likely to be doing in five years' time?

....

....

Use of English: Parts of speech

USE OF ENGLISH

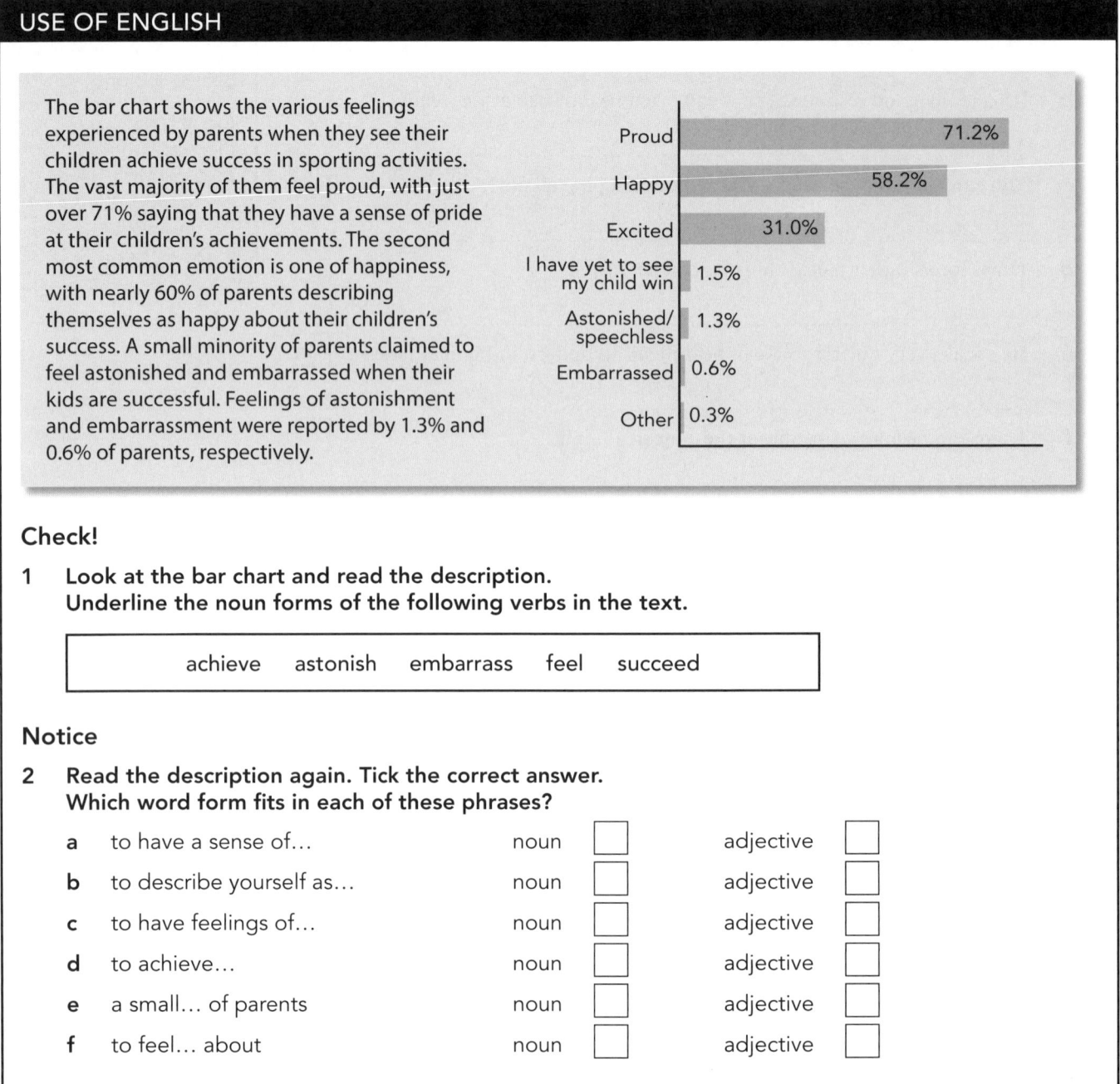

The bar chart shows the various feelings experienced by parents when they see their children achieve success in sporting activities. The vast majority of them feel proud, with just over 71% saying that they have a sense of pride at their children's achievements. The second most common emotion is one of happiness, with nearly 60% of parents describing themselves as happy about their children's success. A small minority of parents claimed to feel astonished and embarrassed when their kids are successful. Feelings of astonishment and embarrassment were reported by 1.3% and 0.6% of parents, respectively.

Check!

1 Look at the bar chart and read the description.
Underline the noun forms of the following verbs in the text.

| achieve   astonish   embarrass   feel   succeed |

Notice

2 Read the description again. Tick the correct answer.
Which word form fits in each of these phrases?

a to have a sense of…   noun ☐   adjective ☐
b to describe yourself as… noun ☐   adjective ☐
c to have feelings of…   noun ☐   adjective ☐
d to achieve…   noun ☐   adjective ☐
e a small… of parents   noun ☐   adjective ☐
f to feel… about   noun ☐   adjective ☐

Focus

3 **Circle the correct word form in each of these sentences.**

a The vast majority of parents had positive feelings about their children's sporting *achievements / achieving*.

b Are you *surprised / surprising* at the reactions of the parents?

c Just over 30% of parents feel a sense of *excited / excitement* at seeing their children do well in sporting activities.

d A small minority of parents have never seen their children *succeed / success* in sport.

e Feelings of *happy / happiness* were reported by nearly 60% of parents.

> **GET IT RIGHT!**
>
> Take care with the spelling of nouns and adjectives.
>
> Example:
> *She was proud of her son's achievements.* (not *achievments*)

Practice

4 Correct the spelling errors in these sentences.

a Stop teasing your brother – you're embarassing him!

b With over 100 published novels, he's a very sucessful author.

c It was a really chalenging match, so we were delighted when we won.

Challenge

5 Look at the bar chart, then complete the description for the bar chart using the correct form of the words in bold.

participate / happy

The bar chart shows the effects of taking part in sport and physical activities on mental health and wellbeing. Just over half of respondents said that ....¹ in physical activities had an impact on their levels of ....².

improve / anxious / energy

Exactly 42% of people felt that there had been an ....³ in their quality of sleep while slightly fewer respondents reported lower levels of ....⁴. 39% of people felt more ....⁵ as a result of doing exercise.

different

Only 14% of people claimed that doing exercise made no positive ....⁶ to their mental health and wellbeing.

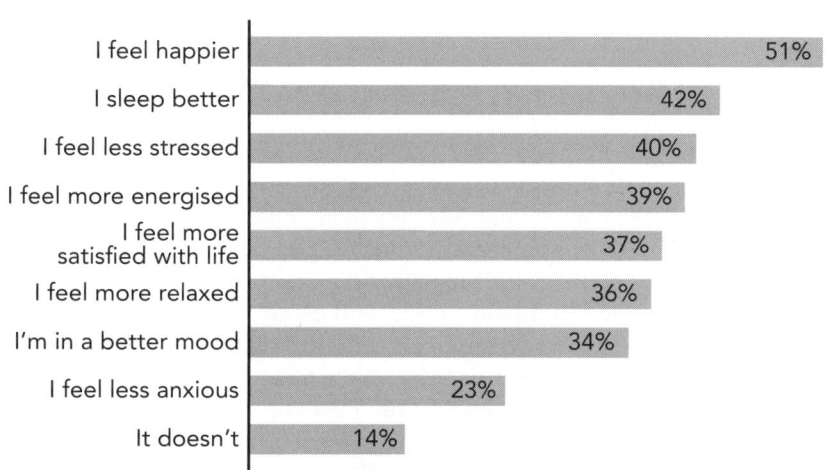

Academic writing: Describing data in charts and graphs

1 Look at the pie chart showing responses to the question 'What do you consider to be the most important aspects of children's sport?'. What aspect of sport do the phrases below refer to?

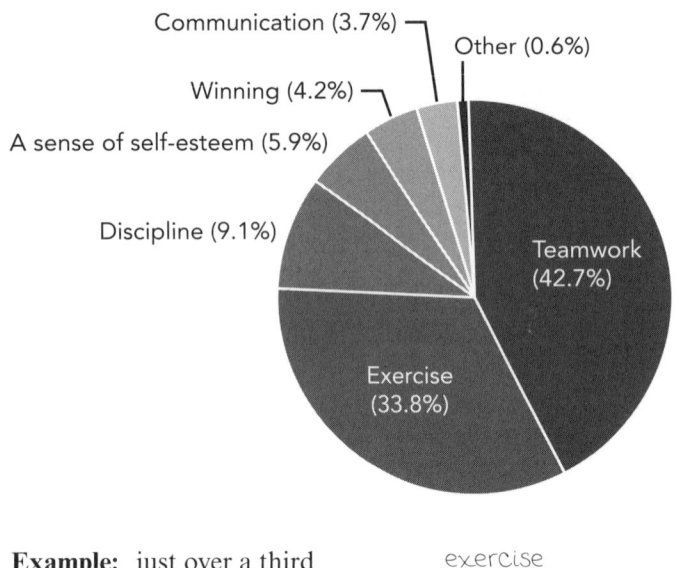

> **WRITING TIP**
>
> Pie charts and bar charts are used to show percentages and proportions. In a description, it is important to use words and phrases to describe percentages and proportions, as well as numbers.

Example: just over a third ......exercise......

a   the most important aspect   ....

b   nearly 6%   ....

c   just under a tenth   ....

d   the least important aspect   ....

e   little difference between   .... and ....

2 Read the following description of the pie chart. Which aspects of sport are mentioned?

> The pie chart shows which aspects of sport parents consider to be most important for their children. Just over 40% of respondents attached particular importance to the role of teamwork in sporting activities. The second most important aspect of taking part in sport was exercise, with just over a third of parents regarding this as the most beneficial reason for participating. Less importance was attached to communication and winning, and there was very little difference in how these were viewed – 3.7% and just over 4%, respectively.
>
> Overall, it is clear that teamwork and exercise were valued more highly by the respondents and that there was comparatively little difference in how parents ranked the importance of the other aspects of sports participation.

3 Read the description again. Underline and label:

a the introductory sentence

b the overview

c a description of the data

d data that supports the description

4 Look at the bar chart showing people's responses to the question 'How do you feel when you win?'. Circle the correct option to complete each statement.

a *Most / Few* people feel a sense of pride when they win.

b *Under a third / Just over a third* of people feel excited at winning.

c There is *very little / considerable* difference between those who feel embarrassed and those who feel unbothered.

d Feelings of happiness were experienced by *little over half / nearly 60%* of people.

5 Write a description of the bar chart from Exercise 4 in your notebook.

Check your progress

Vocabulary

1   Complete the fact files with words and phrases from the box.

> achieved   give up   imperfection   overcome obstacles
> perceived as a failure   resilience   self-esteem   setbacks

Albert Einstein

Physicist Albert Einstein didn't speak for the first three years of his life. But even though he ....1 good grades at school, many of his teachers assumed he was lazy because he was always distracted. He did not let the lack of confidence that many adults had in him affect his ....2. He rose above the negativity and went on to develop the theory of relativity.

Stephen King

Stephen King experienced many ....3 during the early stages of his writing career. His first novel was rejected by 30 different publishers. He was so upset that he threw the manuscript in the bin, but his wife retrieved it and persuaded him not to ....4 on his dream of becoming an author. His books have now sold millions of copies around the world. King's story shows that sometimes people just need a little bit of encouragement to ....5 they encounter in life.

Thomas Edison

Inventor Thomas Edison was ....6 by his teachers and made more than 1000 attempts to invent the light bulb. Through sheer determination and ....7, he succeeded in the end. He took a very constructive view of failure and ....8, and the need to learn from experience, saying: 'Negative results are just what I want. They are just as valuable to me as positive results.'

Grammar

2 Circle the correct word(s) to complete the sentences.

a My keys *could / can't* be in the living room as I've already checked there.

b Remember to wear some old clothes to the farm. The field is really muddy so it's *hardly likely / highly probable* they'll get dirty.

c I'm going to accept the job – I *might / could* not get such a good opportunity again.

d I think she *can / may* like some help with her homework.

e Here's the book I told you about. I think you *can / might* like it.

Reading

3 Skim the article and choose the best title.

A You can mess up and still get ahead!

B The key to success lies in the genes!

> We all want our children to succeed, don't we? What many of us overlook, however, is that allowing them to fail is an important part of any future success. World-class athletes are more able to handle failure than schoolchildren. This is perhaps in part due to the massive commitment they need in order to stay at the top of their game, but is also down to the work carried out by sports psychologists. The difference is that top athletes are often as familiar with their mental states as they are with their physical capabilities.
>
> Stanford University psychologist Carol Dweck believes that success and failure are determined by what the individual understands about themselves, dividing the world into those who have fixed mindsets and those with growth mindsets. Fixed 'mindsetters' are of the opinion that success and failure are genetically programmed into us so that the child who believes themselves to be unintelligent will never be able to succeed academically.
>
> Contrast this with the growth 'mindsetter'. Growth mindsetters view failure as a temporary stop on the way to success, in the same way as an Olympic cyclist views missing out on a medal as an opportunity to assess, improve and get that gold medal next time round.

4 Who might say the following things – someone with a fixed mindset (FM) or a growth mindset (GM)? Circle the correct answers.

a I've never had an aptitude for maths. There's nothing I can do about it.   FM GM

b I didn't finish the paper. I think I may need to work on my speed-reading skills.   FM GM

c I played a terrible match. I don't want to think about it.   FM GM

d I fell over a couple of times on the track but I still finished the race.   FM GM

e I didn't get the job but having the interview was a valuable experience.   FM GM

Writing

5 Write a title for the article in Exercise 3.

REFLECTION

Write answers to these questions in your notebook.

a Choose five key words from this unit and explain why you have chosen them.

b Which famous person in this unit faced the greatest challenge? Why?

c What personal challenges do you think you might have to face in future? Use modals of possibility in your answer.

d Would you describe yourself as a growth mindsetter or a fixed mindsetter? Why?

e Name two things you have learnt about describing information in a bar chart.

3 Then and now

Think about it: The impact of artificial light on insects

1 Read the article about the effect of artificial light on insects.
   Which paragraph of the article contains the following information?

   a one example of a type of light that causes less harm to insects ☐
   b reference to a species that hunts insects ☐
   c the impact of artificial light on insect communication ☐
   d how artificial light can interfere with insect navigation at night ☐
   e reference to the developmental stages of one type of insect ☐

> **porch:** a small area at the entrance to a building, such as a house, that is covered by a roof and often has walls

1 Turn on your **porch** light after sunset, and you will be treated to an aerial display by hundreds of bugs. Artificial lights attract moths, flies, crane flies, mayflies, beetles and all sorts of other insects. You may even find frogs and other insect predators hanging around your porch at night, taking advantage of the easy pickings. […]

2 Night-flying insects evolved to navigate by the light of the moon. By keeping the moon's reflected light at a constant angle, insects can maintain a steady flight path and a straight course. Artificial lights obscure the natural moonlight, making it hard for insects to find their way. […] Since the light bulb radiates light on all sides, the insect simply cannot keep the light source at a constant angle, as it does with the moon. It attempts to navigate a straight path but ends up caught in an endless spiral dance around the bulb.

3 Some scientists believe light pollution is leading to a decline in certain insects. Fireflies, for example, have difficulty identifying the flashes of other fireflies where artificial lights are present. For a moth that lives only a few weeks, a night spent circling a porch light represents a significant chunk of its reproductive lifespan.

4 Another negative impact of artificial lighting on insects is called the 'vacuum cleaner effect', where insects are lured from their normal environment by the draw of the lighting. Mayflies spend their immature stages in water, and finally emerge and develop wings as adults. Their lives are brief, so anything that interferes with mating and egg laying can be disastrous to a given population. [...]

5 Mercury vapor lights are extremely effective at attracting night-flying insects, which is why entomologists use them to observe and capture specimens. If you want to reduce the impact of your outdoor artificial lights on insects, opt for warm colour lights.

2 Read the article again. Which insects does each statement apply to?

a They have a particularly short lifespan. .... and ....

b Their communication signals to potential mates are obscured by artificial light. ....

c The early stages of their lives are spent in water. ....

3 Replace the bold words or phrases in the sentences with a word or phrase from the box.

| detrimental effect   adverse   causal   bringing about |
| overwhelming   correlation |

a Some scientists believe light pollution is **leading to** a decline in insect populations. ....

b The **vast** majority of night-flying insects are attracted to sources of artificial light such as porches.
....

c There is a **clear and established** link between artificial light and the ability of insects to navigate successfully at night.
....

d Warm-coloured light bulbs are considered to have a less **harmful** effect on insects. ....

e There is a direct **relationship** between mercury vapour lights and a decrease in rates of insect reproduction.
....

f One particular **negative impact** of artificial lighting on insects is referred to as the 'vacuum cleaner effect'.
....

Medicine and biology: The effects of stress

1 How stressful do you think each situation is? Grade each one, with 1 not at all stressful and 5 extremely stressful. Write a reason for your answer.

a sitting an exam ☐

....

b riding a rollercoaster ☐

....

c speaking in public ☐

....

d being interviewed for a job ☐

2 Skim the text. Which situation in Exercise 1 is *not* mentioned? ☐

1 Today, we seem to be living in a global Don't Worry Club. Books, magazines, podcasts and TV shows frequently outline the dangers of stress. Many assume that anxious feelings are inherently bad for us in the short and long term – and that they must be **eliminated**.

2 Surprisingly enough, however, a growing body of research suggests that it is our beliefs about our feelings as much as the feelings themselves that determine their effects on the brain and body. Negative views of stress and anxiety often **exacerbate** our problems. And by learning to view these uncomfortable feelings more positively, we may be able to use some forms of stress to our advantage.

3 Let's consider a concrete example. Imagine you are facing a difficult exam or an interview for a job that is going to determine your future career path. If you are like most people, your pulse will speed up, and your rate of breathing might increase too – and you may well assume that this stress response will damage your performance.

4 Now consider an alternative possibility: the 'physiological arousal' that you are experiencing is an evolved response that helps you deal with new challenges. Heavier breathing, for example, fills your lungs with oxygen and the racing pulse ensures that your blood can carry fuel to the brain – changes that should sharpen your thinking.

5 Our attitudes to stress can also alter the way we perceive our environment, and what we learn from it. When faced with a potentially unpleasant task such as public speaking, for example, people who see stress as enhancing are more likely to focus on positive aspects of the scene before them (such as the smiling faces in a crowded room) rather than dwelling on signs of threat or hostility. They also become **proactive** – deliberately seeking feedback and searching for **constructive** ways to cope rather than trying to hide from the problem at hand.

3 Write the bold words in the text next to the correct definitions.

   a to make a situation or problem worse ....

   b having a useful effect rather than being negative or having no purpose ....

   c removed or got rid of ....

   d controlling a situation by making things happen instead of just reacting to events ....

4 Read the text carefully. In which paragraph (1–5) does the writer do the following?

   a describe two physical reactions typically experienced by job interview candidates ☐

   b give examples of media/broadcast sources that focus on the negative effects of stress ☐

   c mention positive and negative perceptions of performing one specific task ☐

   d refer to evidence that challenges existing beliefs about stress ☐

   e suggest that two physical responses to stress may improve mental cognition ☐

Challenge

5 **Research the physical effects that stress can have on the human body, such as making you breathe more heavily. In your notebook, write a list of the positive and negative outcomes these effects have.**

Use of English: *Not only… but also…* and *Neither… nor*

USE OF ENGLISH

Check!

1 Read the sentences about stress. Underline the clauses that include the forms *not only… but also* and *neither… nor*.

   a   Many assume that anxious feelings are neither good for our health in the short term nor beneficial to our wellbeing in the long term.

   b   If you are like most people, not only will your pulse speed up, but also your rate of breathing will increase.

   c   Not only can stress enhance performance, but it can contribute to personal growth too.

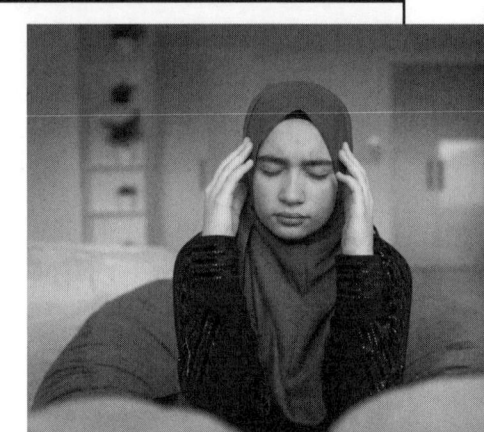

Notice

2 Read the sentences in Exercise 1 again. Answer the questions by circling yes (Y) or no (N).

   a   Is *neither* used with reference to grammatical negatives? Y N

   b   Is *neither* used when something is false for all the people referred to in the sentence? Y N

   c   Does the form *not only* have to be used in the middle of a sentence? Y N

   d   Is there always a comma before the word *but*? Y N

   e   Can the word *too* be used in place of *also*? Y N

Focus

3 **Draw lines to match each phrase (a–e) with a related idea.**

   a   He can play tennis well   i   not economical to drive

   b   She works quickly   ii   didn't apologise

   c   They don't like cats   iii good at football

   d   She didn't remember my birthday   iv   completes every task accurately

   e   Their new car isn't fast   v   hate hamsters

3 Then and now

4 Make sentences using the forms *not only… but also* and *neither… nor*.
Use the phrases and ideas from Exercise 3. The first one has been done for you.

a Not only can he play tennis well, but he is also good at football.

b ....

c ....

d ....

e ....

Practice

5 Find and correct the errors in these sentences. One sentence is correct.

a Not only her kitchen is modern, but it is also spacious.

b Neither of us like the colour purple and nor do we like blue.

c Not only he does paint well, but he also sculpts beautifully.

d He had neither done the homework nor he had brought his books to class.

Challenge

6 Rewrite these sentences using the forms *not only… but also* and *neither… nor* to connect the related ideas. Use the correct form of the verbs in brackets.

a The restaurant manager (didn't give) me a refund (didn't offer) me a discount on my next meal.

....
....

b My sister (write) the film script, she (play) the starring role in the movie.

....
....

c Their physical agility (be) amazing, their mental stamina (be) remarkable.

....
....

d The college (offer) excellent academic courses, it (provide) useful vocational courses.

....
....

GET IT RIGHT!

Remember to invert the order of the subject and the verb in these structures.

Examples:
*Not only **does she** sing beautifully, but she also dances gracefully.*

*We neither saw the castle **nor did we** visit the museum.*

Use of English: Formal conditional structures

USE OF ENGLISH

Check!

1 Underline the examples of conditional forms in these sentences.

   a   Should you have any questions, please get in touch.

   b   If you should see Janos, ask him to call me.

   c   Were you to fail the exam, you would be able to take it next year.

   d   If you have any free time, make sure you visit the castle.

Notice

2   Which three sentences in Exercise 1 contain formal conditional forms? ☐ ☐ ☐

3   Match sentences a–d in Exercise 1 with these statements.

   a   something is unlikely and not particularly plausible ☐ ☐

   b   something is possible and likely ☐ ☐

Focus

4   There is one word missing from each of these sentences. Add the missing word.

   a   Were we turn off all unnecessary lights in our homes, it would lower our energy consumption.

   b   Should wish to help protect insect populations, consider buying yellow light bulbs.

   c   Were the school to put blinds on all classroom windows, it help to reduce light pollution.

   d   you to raise the issue of light pollution with your local council, would they take action?

Practice

5 **Identify and correct the errors in these sentences. Two sentences are correct.**

  a I would never forgive you if you were to mean what you said.

  b If the council were to plant more trees in the neighbourhood, it would be viewed positively by local people.

  c If he were to recognise his mistake, do you think he would admit it?

  d If we were to know more about the council's plans, we would not feel so anxious about the proposed new development.

Challenge

6 **Complete the following sentences in your notebook using formal conditional structures. Write full explanations.**

  a I would study harder if…

  b The area in which I live would be significantly better were the council to…

  c Were I to meet my favourite celebrity in the street…

  d If I could travel anywhere in the world…

> **GET IT RIGHT!**
>
> You can use *if… were* + to infinitive rather than *if* + past simple to talk about imaginary future situations in a more formal way.
>
> Example:
> ***If** the government **were to ban** mercury vapour light bulbs, it could help reverse the decline in insect numbers.*
>
> However, you have to use *if* + past simple with state verbs, such as *belong, doubt, know* and *understand*.
>
> Example:
> *If we understood more about stress, we would be in a better position to deal with it.* (not *we were to understand*)

Academic writing: A proposal

1. Read the task. Underline who you need to write to and the three points you need to cover in your proposal.

> You have been learning about the harmful effects of artificial light on insect species. You feel that your school emits very large amounts of artificial light. You decide to write a proposal to the headteacher outlining some negative impacts of artificial light on insect species, and suggesting some practical ways in which the amount of artificial light could be reduced from inside the school building and on school grounds.

2. Tick three features of proposals.

   A   main heading at the top ☐

   B   subheadings for each paragraph ☐

   C   written in an informal register/style ☐

   D   contains contractions such as (for example, *it's* rather than *it is*) ☐

   E   uses the passive form where possible ☐

3. Read this introduction from a model response to the task in Exercise 1. Underline and label the features of a proposal, including those in Exercise 2.

> **Proposal for the reduction of artificial light on our school premises**
>
> Introduction
>
> We have been studying the adverse effects of artificial light on insect species in our biology class. These include a decline in insect numbers and changes in their behaviour. As large quantities of artificial light are emitted from our school building and outdoor grounds, we would like to suggest some practical ways in which substantial reductions in light emissions could be made.

4. Complete the graphic organiser with your ideas on reducing artificial light from the sports grounds.

Sports ground ← Reducing artificial light at school → **School building**

3 Then and now

5   Look at the student's notes below. Did you come up with any of these ideas in Exercise 4?

> Switch off floodlights after evening matches have been played.
>
> Change the type of lights used.
>
> Reduce the number of floodlights.
>
> Fit the floodlights with a timer so that they switch off automatically.

6   Now note down some suggestions for reducing the amount of artificial light in your school building on the graphic organiser.

7   Read part of a student's answer for this section of the proposal. Did they mention any of your suggestions? Have they followed the advice in Exercise 2?

School building

We would like to suggest that as soon as each floor of the building has been cleaned at the end of the school day, all classroom and corridor lights are turned off. Furthermore, interior lighting casts outdoors, so we propose that blinds are fitted to all windows to minimise the effects of this.

8   Write your own response to the task from Exercise 1 in your notebook. Write 250–300 words. Then complete the checklist.

Have you…

- [ ] covered all the points given in the question?
- [ ] provided a main heading?
- [ ] included subtitles for each paragraph?
- [ ] remembered to use full forms?
- [ ] used the passive form where possible?
- [ ] written in a formal style?
- [ ] written 250–300 words?

Check your progress

Vocabulary

1 **Complete the puzzle using the clues below. What is the mystery word?**

1 different in an interesting way that tests your ability
2 negative and unpleasant
3 the number of times the blood beats in a minute
4 controlling a situation by making things happen
5 remove or get rid of something
6 a connection between two things in which one thing changes as the other does
7 makes a problem worse
8 causing a lot of anxiety and worry
9 having a useful and helpful effect

Mystery word: ....

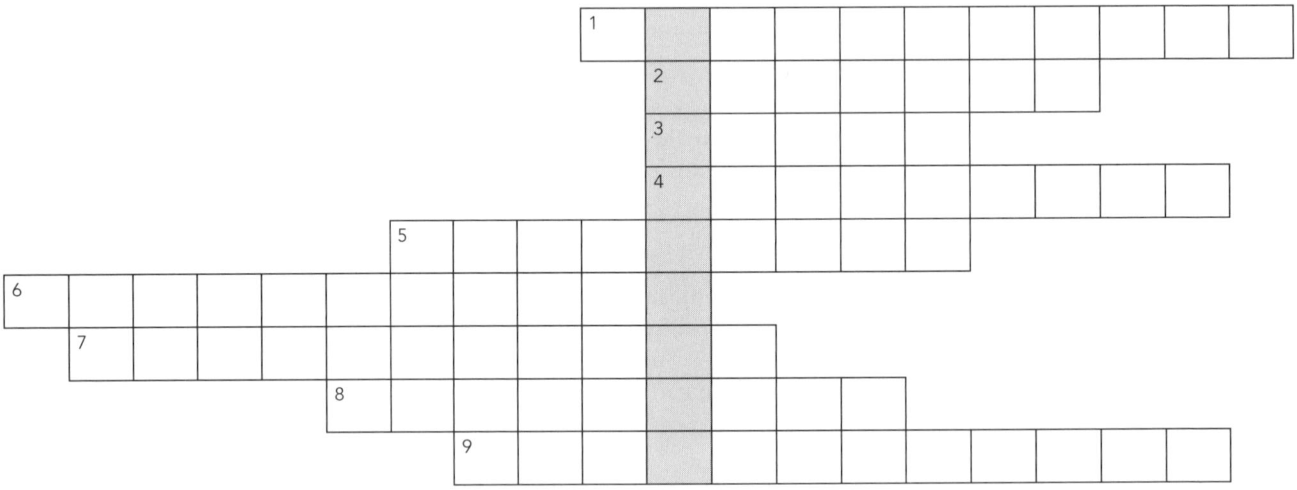

Grammar

2 **Read the text about effective revision.**
Complete the sentences with words from the box to connect the two related ideas.

| give   maintain   help   refresh   ensure   seem |

Be realistic

Break up your revision into chunks so that you know what to study and when. **This will make your revision** ....¹ **less overwhelming and** ....² **it stays manageable.**

Take regular breaks

The human brain can't concentrate for hours at a time. So, take regular breaks – for example, go for a walk or a run. **Spending time away from studying will** ....³ **your mind and** ....⁴ **you stay focused when you return to your desk.**

Find a study group

Revising with other students is a good way to ....⁵ **your social life and** ....⁶ **your morale a much-needed boost.**

3   In your notebook, rewrite the sentences in bold from Exercise 2 using *not only… but also*.

Reading

4   Read the following text quickly. Then answer the questions using one word and/or a number.

   a   How long did the Mausart family live without electronic media? ....

   b   Was the effect on their family life positive or negative? ....

When journalist and commentator Susan Mausart first decided to pull the plug on all electronic media at home, she realised that her children would sooner have volunteered to go without food, water or hair products. At ages 14, 15 and 18, her daughters and son didn't use media. **They inhabited media. Just exactly as fish inhabit a pond. Gracefully. Unblinkingly. And utterly without consciousness or curiosity as to how they got there.**

Susan's experiment with her family was a major success. Her children noticed food more and it even changed their approach to cooking. Her son, for example, taught himself how to grill. Daughter Anni started to read magazines and newspapers for hours at a time. And Susan found that having less to communicate with, her family was communicating more.

At the simplest level, *The Winter of Our Disconnect* is the story of how one family survived six months of wandering through the desert, digitally speaking, and the lessons learnt about themselves and technology along the way. At the same time, their story is a channel to a wider view – into the impact of new media on the lives of families, into the very heart of the meaning of home.

5   Read the text again carefully. Are these statements true (T), false (F) or not given (NG)?

   a   The text is taken from a research journal.
   T   F   NG

   b   The sentences in bold mean that media is a natural part of the children's lives.
   T   F   NG

   c   The family attached less importance to food during their digital detox.
   T   F   NG

   d   The effects of technology on family life merit further attention.   T   F   NG

Writing

6   Read the task and plan your ideas. Then write the proposal in your notebook. Write 250–300 words.

> You have noticed that not many students are using the school library to read and study in. You decide to write a proposal to the headteacher outlining some reasons why the library is not being used and suggest some practical ways in which it could be made more appealing to students.

REFLECTION

Write answers to these questions in your notebook.

   a   Note down three facts you have learnt about the impact of artificial light on insects.

   b   Is there anything that surprised you about the topic of stress? If so, what?

   c   Would you like to take part in a digital detox like the Mausart family? Why or why not?

   d   Look back at your proposal from Exercise 6 and find two places where you could have used a formal conditional structure.

   e   What advice would you give to yourself to improve your skills in writing a proposal?

4 Visual arts

Think about it: Looking at arts and crafts

1 Read the fact file about the artist Picasso. Then match the words in bold in the text with the correct meanings (a–i).

Pablo Picasso

Picasso (1881–1973) was a Spanish painter, sculptor and ceramic artist. He is **universally accepted** as one of the most important artists of the 20th century – developing several new styles of **visual art** and transforming ideas of 'normal' in the art world. Picasso launched an art movement called Cubism, in which shapes of painted human subjects and objects are flattened and simplified, and often painted in sections. These different sections showed all sides of the objects. One of his greatest **masterpieces** is *Guernica*, painted in 1937. One **intrinsic element** of this artwork is the use of black, white and grey paint; Picasso felt these colours represented the horror and destruction of war.

Picasso also created a new type of **sculpture** called 'assemblage', which uses everyday objects and **textiles**. One **concrete example** of this style of art is *The Ape and Her Young*, created in 1951. Picasso used a ball to make the animal's body and his son's toy car was used to make the head.

Picasso also made a wide range of **ceramic art**, including jugs and vases, and he used clay to construct these in the forms of different animal and bird species. It is believed that Picasso visited the prehistoric Altamira Caves in northern Spain in 1934 and was inspired by the **cave paintings** he saw there.

a works of art, such as paintings, that are excellent examples of an artist's work

....

b prehistoric pictures, often showing animals and hunting scenes

....

c objects such as pots made out of clay that have been made permanently hard by heat ....

d figures or objects made by carving or shaping wood, stone, clay or metal

....

e works of art made by weaving or knitting cloth ....

f creative art made to be appreciated by sight, such as painting, sculpture, film-making and architecture ....

g generally agreed by everyone ....

h an example of something that you can see and feel ....

i forming part of the real nature of something ....

VOCABULARY TIP

Visual learners often like to record new vocabulary by drawing a picture. For example, to help remember the word 'sculpture', a visual learner might sketch an image showing this word from the text.

2 **What is the best heading for the text?**

A Taking sole inspiration from traditional artistic techniques

B Challenging conventional definitions of art

3 **Which statement is false according to the text? Circle one.**

Picasso…

A used scenes that evoke conflict

B derived inspiration from common everyday items

C was influenced by very early forms of art

D depicted only animal and bird species in his work

Challenge

4 **Choose a piece of art that you know of or have heard of. Find out more about it, then answer the following questions in your notebook.**

a What is the artwork called? Who created it?

b How does it make you feel when you look at it? Why?

Art: Visual literacy as a life skill

A   **&**   B   **@**   C   **#**   D   ▷

1 Skim the first three paragraphs of the text.
Which symbol (A–D) is being described?

> What does this symbol mean to you? New York's Museum of Modern Art (MOMA) has decided the time is right to honour the 'at' symbol by officially adding the concept to one of its **collections** as a design **icon**.
>
> Writing on MOMA's blog, senior **curator** Paola Antonelli said, 'Physical possession of an object as a requirement for an acquisition is no longer necessary' and that that acknowledgement 'sets curators free to tag the world', whether they are objects too large to bring into the museum or are **abstract concepts**.
>
> The symbol, says Antonelli, has become part of the fabric of life around the world. 'Germans, Poles and South Africans call @ 'monkey's tail' in each different language. Norwegians see a pig's tail, Chinese a little mouse, and Italians and the French, a snail. For Russians, @ **symbolises** a dog, while the Finnish know @ as *miukumauku*, meaning the 'sign of the meow', and believe the symbol is inspired by a curled-up sleeping cat. The @ symbol has become so significant that people feel they need to make sense of it.
>
> According to some linguists, the symbol dates back to the 6th or 7th century, and by 16th-century Venice it referred to an amphora, a measurement vessel used to transport grain and liquid. It first appeared on a typewriter keyboard in 1885 and was eventually selected as a rarely used symbol to separate user names from domain addresses by the American engineer Ray Tomlinson in 1971. He can **take credit for** 'elevating it to defining symbol of the computer age'.

2 Now read the whole text more carefully.
Circle true (T), false (F) or not given (NG) for each of the statements.

    a The text is taken from an article.   T   F   NG

    b The symbol represents the same idea in all languages.   T   F   NG

    c The symbol appeared on the very first typewriter.   T   F   NG

    d Ray Tomlinson experimented with several symbols prior to selecting this symbol.   T   F   NG

4 Visual arts

3 Write the bold words in the text next to the correct definition.

a a person who is in charge of objects and works of art in a museum or gallery

....

b groups of objects – often of the same sort – in museums or galleries

....

c ideas that are not based on one particular person, thing or situation

....

d a thing that people admire and see as a symbol of a particular idea

....

e accept the praise for doing something ....

f represents or is a symbol of something ....

Challenge

4 Choose a word or idea and draw a symbol for it. Explain how it visually represents the idea and why it would be useful.

Use of English: Adjectives modified with extreme adverbs

USE OF ENGLISH

The photographer Christopher Herwig has made an <u>incredibly long</u> journey – more than 30 000 km by car, bike, bus and taxi – through more than ten countries that were once part of the Soviet Union. His aim? To discover and photograph some totally unexpected treasures of modern art – bus stops. The diversity of the architectural designs he comes across is absolutely extraordinary! They include bus stops shaped as trains, birds, light bulbs, rockets and castles. These structures show the extremely wide range of public art from the Soviet era and give an utterly fascinating insight into the creative minds of the sculptors, architects and builders who designed and constructed them.

Check!

1 Underline examples of adjectives modified with extreme adverbs in the text above. One example has been given.

Notice

2 Tick the three correct statements.

Extreme adverbs…

A change the strength of adjectives ☐

B are placed before adjectives ☐

C include 'quite' and 'slightly' ☐

D must be followed by a comma ☐

E emphasise a speaker/writer's feelings about something ☐

4 Visual arts

Focus

3 Circle the correct extreme adverbs to complete the sentences.

a   It was *an utterly / extremely* hot day yesterday. I had to keep drinking water to cool down.

b   It's *absolutely / completely* freezing today. Whatever you do, don't forget your hat and gloves when you go out!

c   She's *a totally / an extremely* unique artist. I've never seen paintings like hers before.

d   Thanks for such a lovely present. It's *extremely / utterly* perfect – exactly what I wanted.

e   He is known for creating *incredibly / totally* large metal sculptures.

f   I *completely / extremely* agree that she was one of the most influential artists of the 20th century.

> **GET IT RIGHT!**
>
> Adjectives like *amazing, awful* and *boiling* contain the idea of 'very' in their definitions. To emphasise the strength of these adjectives, you need to use *absolutely* or *really*.
>
> Example:
> *Summers in my country are **absolutely boiling***.
> (not *very* or *extremely* boiling)

Practice

**4 There is an error in some of these sentences.
Find the error in each sentence and correct it. One sentence is correct.**

a   It's the worst film I've ever seen – it's absolutely bad!

b   It was a great match, and everyone played extremely well.

c   The rail service is very fantastic where I live. Trains always depart and arrive on time.

d   I heard she got the job, which is totally good news!

e   That cake you baked for me was very amazing. I really enjoyed it!

f   I extremely agree with you – it was a very disappointing concert.

Challenge

5 What do you think about the bus stops in the pictures in this lesson? Which one would you most like to stand at? Why? Write down your ideas in your notebook, using adjectives modified by extreme adverbs.

Use of English: Impersonal passive reporting verbs

USE OF ENGLISH

Check!

1 Underline examples of the passive form in these sentences.

   a It is considered to be one of his greatest masterpieces.

   b Many of her famous artworks have been copied and reproduced.

   c Each object has to be catalogued prior to going on display at the exhibition.

   d It is unknown who the creator of this painting is – it's a complete mystery.

Notice

2 Match the examples of the passive (a–d) in Exercise 1 with the reasons for using it (i–iv) below.

   i   The sentence focuses on the action. ☐

   ii   The person doing the action is not known or is unimportant. ☐ and ☐

   iii Generally held opinions are being expressed. ☐

   iv   The sentence is describing a process. ☐

Focus

3 **Rewrite these sentences with an impersonal *it* using the correct form of the verbs in brackets.**

   a People say that the @ sign dates from the 6th or 7th century. (say)

   ....

   b Ray Tomlinson sent the first email in 1971. (know)

   ....

   c People consider the @ sign to be an example of visual art. (consider)

   ....

   d People used amphorae to transport grain and liquid in the 16th century. (believe)

   ....

> **GET IT RIGHT!**
>
> Remember to use the correct form of the verb *to be*.
>
> It + be + verb + that
>
> Example:
> It **was** thought that the painting had been stolen. (not *were*)
>
> Subject + be + reporting verb + infinitive
>
> Example:
> It **is** thought **to be** one of the best examples of ceramic art. (not *being*)

Practice

4 Add the missing word to each of these sentences.

a It painted in the early 20th century.

b It is widely thought be one of the finest pieces of ceramic art.

c The artwork was stolen but it subsequently returned safely to the museum.

d It was initially believed to a fake but it turned out to be genuine.

Challenge

5 Complete each gap in the text using a verb from the box in the correct form.

| believe   call   inspire   paint   think   write about |

What is Surrealist art?

Surrealism is an exciting and unusual form of art. It makes people see things in a different way and it can ....¹ by an artist's dreams or by putting strange objects together in unexpected groups. Surrealism ....² to have started in Paris, France in the 1920s and ....³ by a French poet called André Breton. It ....⁴ that he was very interested in the thoughts, dreams and unusual ideas artists had, rather than just life-like recreations of everyday things. One of the most famous examples from this period ....⁵ by the German artist Max Ernst. It ....⁶ *Two Children Are Threatened by a Nightingale*.

Academic writing: An argument essay

1 **Look at the two photographs and answer these questions.**

   a   What do you think the students are learning about?

   b   What skills are they developing?

   c   What do you think they are enjoying about learning in these different ways? Why?

2 **Read the essay question. Underline the thesis statement.**

Trips to museums and art galleries should be a compulsory part of school programmes because they offer many educational benefits for students. Do you agree?

3 **Put the steps below in the flowchart in the best order for writing an argumentative essay.**

> Consider the opposing point of view.
> Explain why you disagree with the opposing view.
> Express your opinion clearly in the introduction.
> Rephrase the essay question in your own words.
> Restate your opinion in the conclusion.
> Support your opinion with examples.

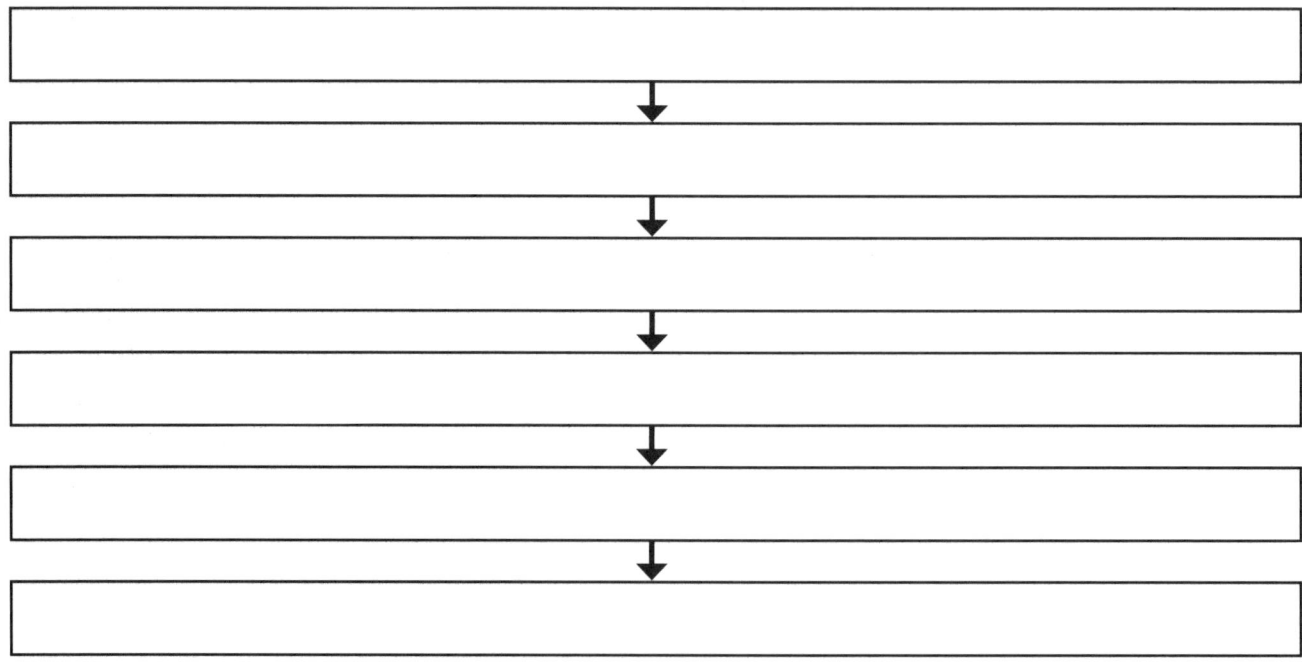

4 **Visual arts**

4 Look at the useful words in the box for presenting different views on a topic. Complete the sentences using these words.

> believe   extent   view   argued

- **a** It can be .... that students can develop important thinking skills. By looking closely at a painting in an art gallery, for example, they can speculate about how the artist created it and why.

- **b** I firmly .... that students enjoy a far wider range of stimuli than they would be exposed to in a classroom. These include the opportunity to touch artefacts and consider how they would have been used.

- **c** Some people, such as parents and teachers, take the .... that students need to focus more time on preparing for exams and that this is best done within the confines of a classroom.

- **d** To a large .... going on a visit to a gallery can provide a welcome change from the normal routine and format of lessons.

5 Which sentence in Exercise 4 disagrees with the thesis statement in the essay question? ☐

6 Read these sentences from the conclusion to an argumentative essay. Put the sentences into the correct order.

- **a** Young people undoubtedly benefit from acquiring knowledge from a variety of sources and so trips to museums and galleries should form an integral part of their learning. ☐

- **b** In conclusion, I firmly believe that museums and art galleries provide a unique window on the world. ☐

- **c** By giving students the opportunity to look through these windows on a regular basis, they will begin to understand how the world changes over time, and why. ☐

7 Complete the graphic organiser with your own ideas about the essay question.

8 Write your own response to the essay question in your notebook. Write about 350 words.

Check your progress

Vocabulary

1 Complete the puzzle using the clues below. What is the mystery word?

1 a very impressive work of art
2 to show something, especially in a picture
3 something that someone buys to add to what they already own
4 someone who makes objects such as vases and jugs out of clay (2 words)
5 a person in charge of the objects in a museum or art gallery
6 art forms such as painting, drawing, photography and design (2 words)
7 a famous thing that people admire and see as a symbol of a particular idea

Mystery word: ....

Grammar

2 Circle the correct extreme adverbs to complete the text.

Picasso's *Guernica*

I can't take my eyes off this image – it's *utterly / extremely*¹ powerful, even though the colours are *totally / really*² simple, just grey, white and black. You can see how *very / incredibly*³ terrified the people and animals are feeling. The artist captures the destruction of war *absolutely / extremely*⁴ perfectly.

3 Complete the gaps in the text with an appropriate passive form.

An ampersand (&) is a symbol that represents the word *and*. It ....¹ (think) to have been around for nearly 2000 years. Although it ....² (not know) who invented it, it ....³ (believe) that the symbol was drawn on a wall in Pompeii before Mount Vesuvius erupted in 79 CE. In 19th-century Britain, the ampersand ....⁴ (consider) to be part of the alphabet. It was the 27th letter and it ....⁵ (pronounce) as 'and'. To differentiate it from letters, students would use the phrase 'per se' meaning 'by itself', so they would end the alphabet by saying 'x, y, z and per se 'and''. Nowadays, the ampersand ....⁶ (use) in trademark names such as 'Johnson & Johnson' and in the titles of films, such as *Marley & Me*.

Reading

4 Skim the paragraph. Who is the intended audience?

A university researchers
B educators
C parents

> Visual literacy has always been important in the lives of humans. The ability to interpret and create images goes back to the earliest civilisations. The 21st century has also created its own set of visual symbols such as the thumbs-up 'like' button or the smiling emoticon. But if we want to understand the real importance of visual literacy skills, consider the long list of new words which have entered the English language in the last ten years. They include **infographic, mashup, binge-watch, augmented reality, meme, emoji**. All these new words connect in some way to the use of modern visual stimuli.
>
> As teachers we've all used pictures and videos in our lessons and know the value they bring to language learning. However, in an age where we have so much access to images and the ability to create and share our own, it's worth asking ourselves if we are really exploiting the full potential of our students' visual literacy.

5 Which statement best corresponds with the ideas in the text?

A Young people have a better understanding of visual literacy than teachers.
B A wide range of visual stimuli is waiting to be exploited.

Writing

6 Read the essay question. Underline the key words.

The best places for students to appreciate art and develop visual literacy skills are not in classrooms but in outdoor settings such as sculpture parks and gardens. Do you agree?

7 Write a response to the essay question in your notebook. Consider the following questions.

- What might be the advantages and disadvantages of learning about art in outdoor locations such as sculpture parks and gardens?
- Would you prefer to enjoy art inside a classroom or outdoors? Why?

REFLECTION

Write answers to these questions in your notebook.

a Choose five interesting words or phrases from this unit and draw pictures to represent their meanings.
b Name three things you have learnt about the artist Picasso.
c How would you explain the meaning of visual literacy in clear, simple terms?
d Some people say that symbols communicate better than words. What do you think?
f Look back at your last essay and find two places where you could have used the *it* passive form.

5 The benefits and risks of artificial intelligence (AI)

Think about it: The role of AI in customer service

1   Read the article, then match the words in bold in the text with the definitions (a–d).

I arrive at 2.55 p.m. All is quiet. Behind reception is a motionless but lifelike girl robot wearing a cream jacket and a smirk. She has a sign saying 'only Japanese', so I approach another robot, this one designed, bizarrely, to look like a velociraptor and wearing a bow tie and a hat. I say hello. Nothing. I wave and he stares past me, his arms outstretched but unmoving.

'I'd like to check in please,' I shout, wondering if the robots are <u>voice-activated</u>. A door opens and a real live human in a black T-shirt appears. 'Check-in is 3 p.m.,' he says, and goes back into his room.

Robots are taking off in Japan and several companies manufacture them to perform a range of **functions**. There are <u>humanoid</u> robots on reception in banks and robots guide visitors around the capital's National Museum of Emerging Science and Innovation. The hotel's owner says he wants to make this 'the most efficient hotel in the world' by reducing manpower and having 90% of staff be <u>robotic</u>.

At 3 p.m. the velociraptor comes to life and says, in an American accent, 'Welcome to the Henn-na hotel. If you want to check in, press one.' I start tapping the screen but the man in black appears again and asks for my passport, leaving the robot to fall into a state of inertia. How disappointing.

The hotel's other robots include a giant mechanical arm in a glass case that stores luggage in individual drawers for ¥500 (£2.50). There's also a foot-high 'concierge' who is pre-programmed to explain breakfast times and order taxis.

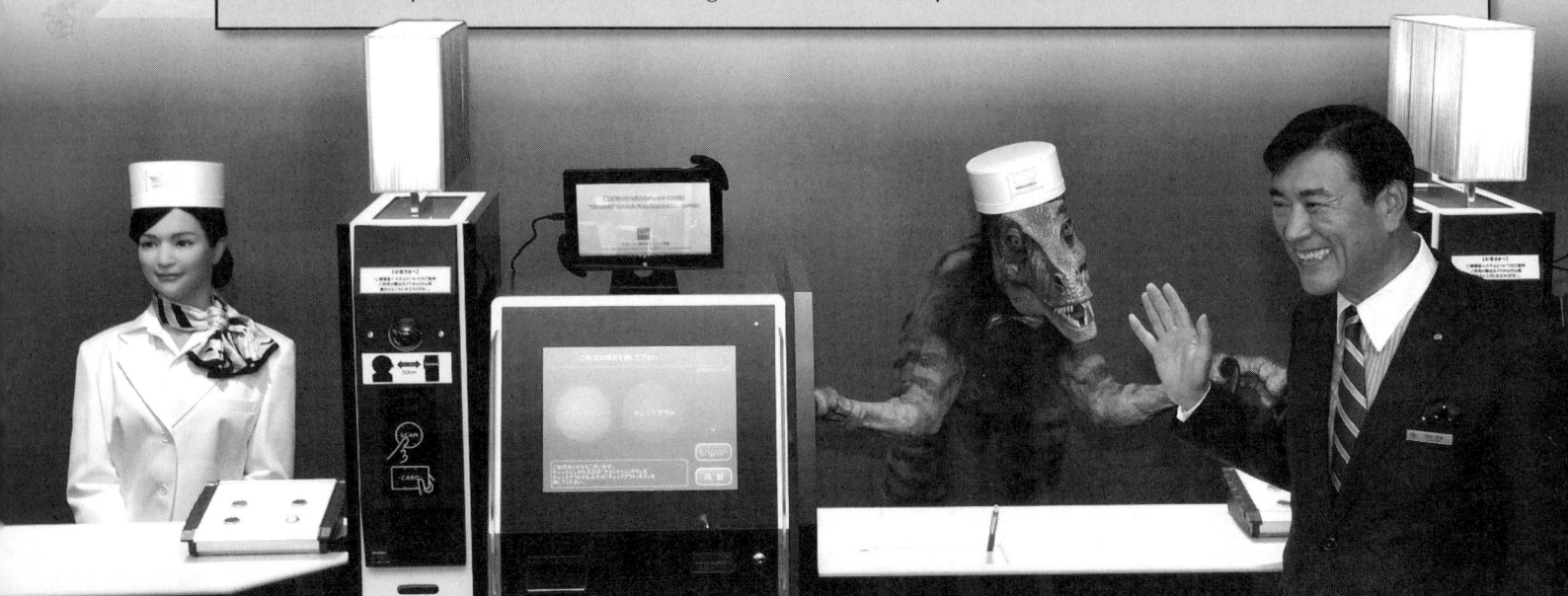

5 The benefits and risks of artificial intelligence (AI)

> Robot 'porters' are two rechargeable luggage trolleys – but only for residents of one luxury part of the hotel.
>
> Using facial recognition software, I let myself into my room and find, on my bedside table, Chu-ri-chan, a cute little electronic creature.
>
> She will perform **automated tasks** which include switching on the lights, offering weather forecasts and wake-up calls. She'll also perk up after being silent for an hour and then **trigger** into action, scaring the life out of you. Robots may be the future, but for hotel hospitality, you still can't beat the human touch.

a   work activities completed using computer software   ....

b   operations performed in a particular way   ....

c   cause a machine or device to start functioning   ....

> **VOCABULARY TIP**
>
> It's a good idea to record the different forms of related words. For example, the words *robot*, *robotic* and *robotics* all relate to the same word family. Noting them down together will help you to remember how they are used.

2   **Write definitions for the underlined words and phrases in the article.**

   a   humanoid

   ....

   b   robotic

   ....

   c   facial recognition software

   ....

3   **Which of the following best describes the writer's view of the customer service in the robot hotel?**

   A   completely positive   **B**   a little negative   **C**   entirely neutral

4   **Read the article again. Circle the correct answer – yes (Y) or no (N).**

   a   Both hotel reception robots speak two languages.   Y N

   b   The writer completes the check-in process without human intervention.   Y N

   c   Additional charges apply to the use of the mechanical arm robot.   Y N

   d   Robot porters are available to assist all guests in the hotel.   Y N

Challenge

5   **Write an advertisement for the robot hotel, explaining what makes it different to a stay in a conventional hotel.**

Computer science: Human–robot interaction

1 Read the article, then answer the questions.

> 1. Laughter comes in many forms, from a chuckle to a howl of **mirth**. Scientists are now developing an AI system that aims to recreate these **nuances** of humour by laughing in the right way at the right time. The team behind the laughing robot, which is called Erica, say that the system could improve natural conversations between people and AI systems.
>
> 2. 'We think that one of the most important functions of conversational AI is empathy,' said Dr Koji Inoue, of Kyoto University, the lead author of the research. 'So, we decided that one way a robot can empathise with users is to share their laughter.' Inoue and his colleagues have set out to teach their AI system the art of conversational laughter.
>
> 3. The research team gathered training data from more than 80 dialogues between male university students and the robot, who was initially <u>tele-operated</u> by four female amateur actors.
>
> 4. The dialogue data was annotated for solo laughs, social laughs (where humour isn't involved, such as polite or embarrassed laughter) and the laughter of mirth. The data was then used to train a machine learning system to decide whether to laugh, and to choose the appropriate type. Based on the audio files, the <u>algorithm</u> learnt the basic characteristics of social laughs, which tend to be more **subdued**, and mirthful laughs, with the aim of <u>imitating</u> these in appropriate situations.
>
> 5. The team created four short dialogues for Erica to share with a person, integrating the new shared-laughter algorithm into existing <u>conversation software</u>. These were compared to scenarios where Erica didn't laugh at all or emitted a social laugh every time she detected laughter. The clips were played to 130 volunteers who rated the shared-laughter algorithm most favourably for empathy, naturalness, human-likeness and understanding.
>
> 6. The team said laughter could help create robots with their own distinct character. 'We think that they can show this through their conversational behaviours, such as laughing, eye gaze and gestures,' said Inoue.

mirth: laughter, humour or happiness

nuances: very slight differences in appearance, meaning or sound

subdued: not strong or loud

5   The benefits and risks of artificial intelligence (AI)

In which paragraph (1–6) does the writer:

a   mention three types of laughs categorised by the research team? ☐

b   provide a set of criteria used to evaluate Erica in the research study? ☐

c   describe some non-verbal behaviour associated with the art of conversation? ☐

d   explain who participated in the dialogues with Erica? ☐

2   **Which two statements are true, according to the article?**

Social laughter…

A   centres around humour ☐

B   tends to be emitted quietly ☐

C   conveys empathy with other people ☐

D   may be produced when someone feels uncomfortable ☐

E   can be rude in tone ☐

3   **Read the text again. What do the following numbers refer to?**

4   ....

80   ....

130   ....

4   **Write definitions for the underlined words and phrases in the article.**

a   tele-operated

....

b   algorithm

....

c   imitating

....

d   conversation software

....

Challenge

5   **In your notebook, write down three ways that conversational robots might be useful in society.**

Use of English: Rhetorical questions

USE OF ENGLISH

Will AI take over the world?

Currently the AI we have developed is only good for achieving very specific tasks, such as playing a game of chess or driving a car, and requires a great deal of human involvement. However, there is a very real possibility that in the future we could reach what is known as 'the singularity', where AI develops general intelligence and becomes smarter than humans. This would mean, no doubt, that the singularity would have a big impact on human civilisation. So, does that mean we should we worried about the future of humankind? Well, the good news is there are several organisations, such as the Machine Intelligence Research Institute and the Future of Life Institute, focusing on keeping AI safe and beneficial for humans.

Check!

1 Underline the two rhetorical questions in the text.

Notice

2 Why did the writer decide to use rhetorical questions in the text? Tick two reasons.

   A to make a statement without expecting an answer ☐

   B to engage the reader's interest before they read further ☐

   C to lead into/introduce their point of view ☐

Focus

3 Match the rhetorical questions (a–c) with the correct statements (i–iii).

   a Could AI systems end up taking over the world?

   b Do you think that robots will ever be able to perform all jobs in the workplace?

   c Can AI ever replicate human communication?

   i   Absolutely not – especially when it comes to conveying empathy and humour.

   ii Read on to find out whether they will have global dominance in future.

   iii Experts are divided about which areas of employment may be at risk.

5 The benefits and risks of artificial intelligence (AI)

4 Which rhetorical question in Exercise 3 (a–c) introduces the writer's personal point of view? ☐

GET IT RIGHT!
Remember that you need to invert the subject and the auxiliary verb when writing rhetorical questions.

Example:
Could AI systems end up taking over the world? (not *AI systems could*)

Practice

5 Some of these rhetorical questions are incorrect. Correct the errors where necessary. One rhetorical question is correct.

a You can imagine travelling in a driverless car?

b Would you ever consider staying in a robot hotel?

c You are interested in finding out more about facial recognition software?

d You think robots will ever be able to understand what we are thinking?

6 Write your own responses to the rhetorical questions in Exercise 5.
Try to give a full answer to each one, stating your personal point of view.

a ....

b ....

c ....

d ....

Challenge

7 Look at the areas of life that will be affected by AI in the future. Choose one topic from the list and write a short paragraph about it. Include two rhetorical questions – one to engage the interest of your reader and the other to give your personal point of view.

- education
- communication
- leisure time
- medicine
- travel and transport

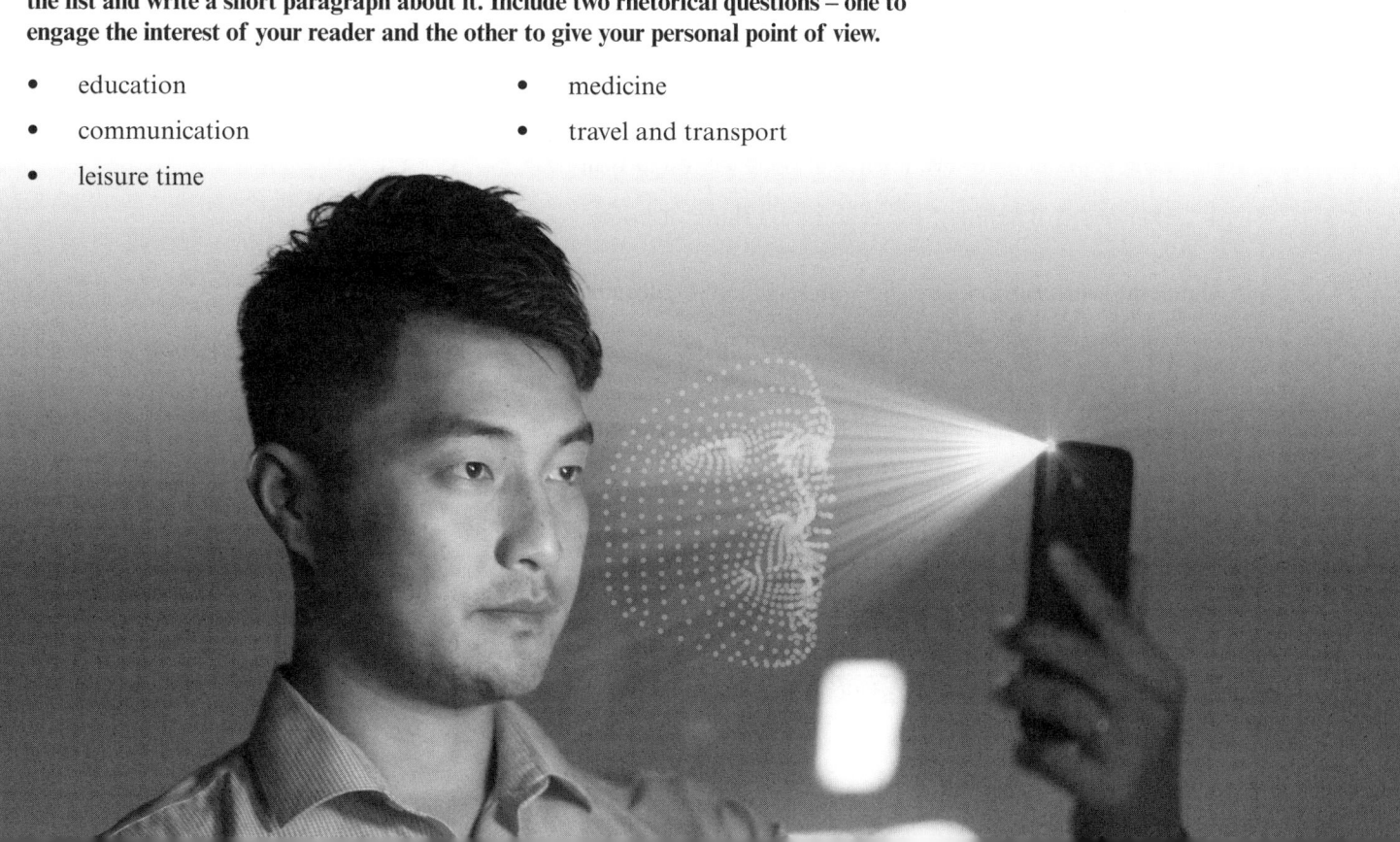

Use of English: Subordinating conjunctions

USE OF ENGLISH

Check!

1 Tick the two true statements about the form, meaning and use of subordinating conjunctions.

Subordinating conjunctions…

A are used to emphasise a writer's feeling about something ☐

B always appear at the beginning of a sentence ☐

C are used to mean 'it doesn't matter what/where/how/where' ☐

Notice

2 Read these sentences and underline the subordinating conjunctions.

a Whatever people say, robots are here to stay.

b CCTV cameras are watching you wherever you go.

c However you try to justify your opinion about driverless cars, others will still disagree with you.

d Whenever we go out together, it's always a lot of fun.

Focus

3 Circle the correct subordinating conjunction to complete each sentence.

a *Whatever / However* you say, I won't change my mind.

b *However / Whenever* we meet, we always have plenty to talk about.

c Robots are here to stay, *whenever / however* you look at it.

d *Whenever / Whatever* I travel abroad, I think of home.

4 Match the sentences in Exercise 3 with their correct meanings below.

i Any time we get together we're never short of things to say to each other. ☐

ii Even if it may be tempting to think otherwise, they are the future. ☐

iii No matter where I happen to be in the world – it's just something I tend to do. ☐

iv It makes no difference what you tell me. ☐

5 The benefits and risks of artificial intelligence (AI)

Practice

5 **Correct the errors in the sentences below. One sentence is correct.**

a Whenever I travel I always call my family back home.

b What ever decision you make, I will support you.

c Whereever we look, we see busy people rushing around.

d How ever hard I try, I can't make sense of this homework.

e Whatever can she be doing? She's been upstairs for ages.

6 **Complete the sentences with the words from the box.**

| However | Whatever | Whenever | Wherever | Whoever |

a .... she wears, she always looks good.

b .... you're free, I can meet you. Just say when and where!

c .... many times you tell me, I always forget your phone number.

d .... is in charge of the restaurant, could you put me through to them please? I want to make a complaint.

e .... they can find work, they'll move there.

GET IT RIGHT!

Make sure you are spelling subordinating conjunctions correctly. For example, *wherever*, not *where ever* or *whereever*.

Remember also to put a comma at the end of the clause when you use a subordinating conjunction at the beginning of a sentence.

Example:
Wherever they go, they always meet interesting people.

Challenge

7 **In your notebook, write four pieces of advice for someone about how to stay safe online. Use subordinating conjunctions where possible to focus your reader on the information that follows.**

Whenever you're online, make sure your privacy settings are on.

Academic writing: An agree/disagree essay

1 Do you think humans will be replaced by robots in the jobs below in the future? Put 1 for strongly agree, 2 for partially agree, 3 for partially disagree or 4 for strongly disagree. Note down reasons for your answers in your notebook.

shop assistant ☐   teacher ☐
truck driver ☐   pilot ☐
firefighter ☐   football manager ☐
paramedic ☐   film director ☐

2 Read the essay question. Tick the two correct statements about agree/disagree essays.

'Robots will replace all human jobs in future.'
To what extent do you agree with this statement?

A You can partially agree with the statement. ☐

B You should avoid stating your opinion in the introduction. ☐

C You need to say what you think about the statement at the end of your essay. ☐

3 Read part of a student's answer to the essay question in Exercise 2. Ignore the gaps for now. Which job from Exercise 1 do they mention? Does the student share the same opinion as you about the future of this job?

> There is no doubt that we are living in an increasingly automated world and this is having a profound impact on how a wide range of jobs are ......¹. However, it is important to remember that some occupations are more at risk of automation than others. The ones most likely to be replaced by robots are those jobs that involve performing routine, repetitive and predictable activities. Fast-food cooks, for example, carry out highly predictable tasks. AI-powered kitchen assistants can be easily ......² with a high level of efficiency. Long-distance lorry drivers are also vulnerable to losing their jobs to AI systems. Automated vehicles do not require lunch breaks or sleep in order to function. This means that accidents ......³ are likely to be completely eliminated.
>
> However, it is important to remember that some jobs will remain comparatively safe from robots. These include jobs that involve genuine creativity, such as the work ......⁴. Although it is true to say that computers have already ......⁵ and orchestral works, humans are still best at creativity, and I cannot see that changing in future. Moreover, occupations that involve building solid relationships with people, for instance dentists, are unlikely to be ......⁶. Robots simply do not have the emotional intelligence or the communication skills ......⁷ in an empathetic way. Finally, jobs that involve responding to emergency situations in real time are likely to be relatively safe from robots. For example, a plumber ......⁸ in an emergency in the middle of the night would be extremely difficult to replace with an automated robot.

4   Complete the model essay in Exercise 3 with the phrases below. Write the correct letter in each gap. Then read it again and underline useful phrases.

    a   pre-programmed to flip burgers
    b   done by artists and musicians
    c   carried out in the workplace
    d   replaced with AI systems
    e   caused by human drivers on the road
    f   needed to fix a burst pipe
    g   required to interact with humans
    h   produced high-quality paintings

5   Read the model essay again. To what extent does the student agree with the statement in the essay question?

    A   strongly agree ☐
    B   partially agree ☐
    C   strongly disagree ☐

6   Write a conclusion that reflects the views of the writer of the model essay. Begin with 'In conclusion' or 'To conclude'.

7   Using your own ideas about the jobs in Exercise 1, write a response to the essay question from Exercise 2.

Check your progress

Vocabulary

1 **Match the two parts of each sentence to make definitions.**

a An algorithm

b AI

c Facial recognition software

d Robotics

e Automated tasks

f The singularity

i describe routine, repetitive activities performed by machines and robots.

ii is the science of designing and operating robots.

iii refers to a technology capable of matching a human face from a digital image against a database of faces.

iv describes a future scenario in which AI develops general intelligence and becomes smarter than humans.

v is an area of study concerning making computers copy intelligent human behaviour.

vi can be defined as a process or set of instructions to be followed by a computer.

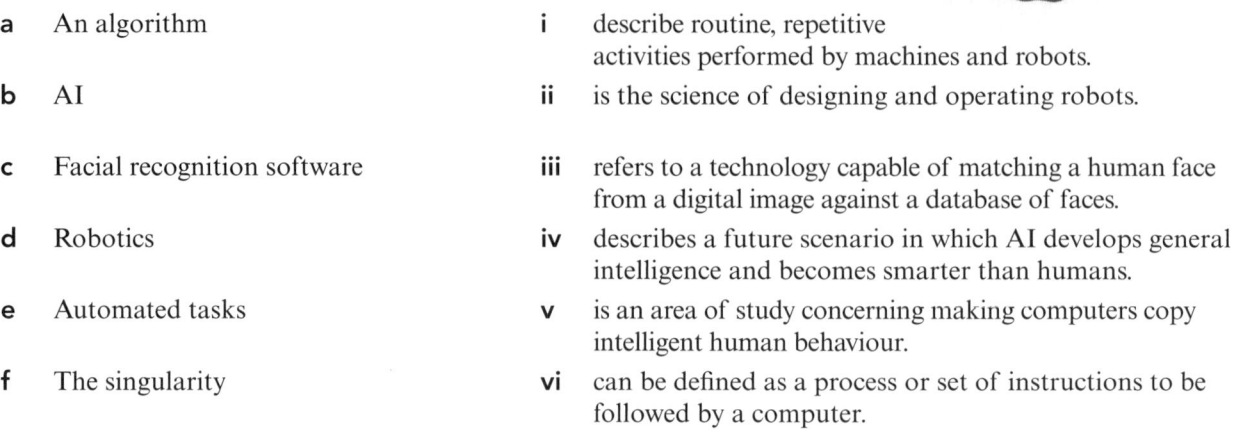

Grammar

2 **Create rhetorical questions as headings for these short texts, using the prompts provided. The first one has been done for you.**

a **Question: AI / flights safer?**

Could AI systems help make flights safer?

Tests are already underway on autonomous planes that take off, cruise and land with very little human input. Most air passengers are fairly comfortable with autopilot technology.

b **Question: AI / bad weather conditions?**

....

Researchers are working on the use of 'hyper-imaging' and AI. This tech will be used in cars to help drivers see through heavy fog and other adverse weather.

c **Question: AI / skin cancer?**

....

Using images from a smartphone, AI can spot signs of skin cancer then diagnose conditions with the accuracy of a dermatologist.

d **Question: AI / human hearts?**

....

Using human tissue, 3D printing can produce body parts and organs. Printed ears and noses have already been transplanted and in future miniature hearts could be printed.

3 **Complete these sentences with an appropriate subordinating conjunction.**

a .... you want to do, I'm happy to go along with it.

b .... many times I try, I just can't seem to get it right!

c .... I can find the time, I go walking in the mountains.

d .... I go, I always take my phone with me.

66

Reading

4 Skim the text below. Tick the best title.

A Driverless vehicles – pros and cons ☐

B A personal account of travelling in a self-driving car ☐

C Advantages of automated vehicles ☐

> A study carried out at a university in the USA has shown that simply having a few autonomous vehicles on the roads could significantly reduce traffic problems. The researchers discovered that driverless cars are an advantage for other road users. This is partly because they drive smoothly and at a careful speed, both of which help to improve the flow of traffic. The data suggested that there would be fewer accidents if a mere 5% of vehicles on the roads were autonomous. There would also be fewer stop-go traffic circumstances, and a big decrease in fuel consumption – up to 40%.

5 What three benefits of driverless vehicles does the writer mention?

....

....

....

Writing

6 Write answers to the following questions in your notebook.

a Would you like to be a passenger in a driverless vehicle? Why or why not?

b What possible disadvantages could there be with driverless vehicle technology?

7 Read the essay question and underline the key words. Then write the essay in your notebook. You may wish to consider the following jobs:

- pilot
- air-traffic controller
- train driver
- astronaut
- travel writer
- tourist guide.

'Robots and AI systems will take over all jobs in the areas of travel and transport in future.'

To what extent do you agree with this statement?

REFLECTION

Write answers to these questions in your notebook.

a Choose five key words that you think best summarise this unit.

b What are three facts that you learnt about the robot hotel?

c Some people say that in the future robots will be able to understand us. What do you think? Why?

d What have you learnt about the effects of AI on travel and transport? Make brief notes on the possible advantages and disadvantages.

e Look back at your essay and find two places where you could have used rhetorical questions.

6 What it is to be human

Think about it: The secrets of a long and healthy life

1 Complete the questions with words from the box. Then match them with answers i–viii.

> centenarians   cholesterol   detrimental   life expectancy
> physiological benefits   protein   sedentary lifestyle   whole grains

a What is the average .... in the world?

b Which country has the highest number of ....?

c What are the possible side effects of having too much ....?

d How much .... do humans need in their diet?

e Why is eating too much fast food .... to our health?

f What are the .... of doing exercise regularly?

g What are the health risks of living a ....?

h Why are .... considered a healthy part of our diet?

i   High blood pressure and risk of heart attack and stroke. ☐

ii 0.8 grams per kilogram of body weight. ☐

iii They contain many unhealthy ingredients like sugar, trans fats and sodium. ☐

iv It increases the risk of high blood pressure and heart disease. ☐

v   They are a good source of fibre, vitamins, minerals and other nutrients. ☐

vi It keeps your heart healthy and prevents you from being overweight. ☐

vii 0.06% of the population in Japan is aged 100 or older. ☐

viii It has risen consistently over the last few decades and is now just over 73. ☐

2   Read the paragraph and answer the questions in your own words.

Diet and longevity

There are many factors that affect life expectancy, including environmental and genetic factors, but there is mounting evidence that diet plays a significant role. A recent longitudinal study of 2400 people spanning a period of 11 years suggests that consuming a Mediterranean diet that is rich in fruits, vegetables and healthy fats may enhance our ability to resist age-related diseases. The theory was corroborated by another study, which found that people who changed their diet to include more whole grains, legumes and nuts can increase their life expectancy by up to eight years.

a   What did both studies aim to find out?

    ....

b   Why is the first study described as a 'longitudinal' study?

    ....

c   What is the relationship between the second study and the first study?

    ....

d   What other factors not mentioned in the text do you think might affect life expectancy?

    ....

3   Read the text again. Write a summary in your notebook using 50 words or fewer.

History and economics: An edible history

1 Look at the photos. What food is shown in each picture?

A

B

C

....

2 Match three different descriptions to each type of food.
Write the correct letters from Exercise 1.

a It was considered so precious that it was equal in value to gold and ivory. It was transported by **maritime** trade routes from Indonesia to East Africa, where Arab traders took it north into Egypt. There it was sold to Venetian traders, who held a monopoly on the trade in Europe.

b It was first grown in China as long as 10 000 years ago and is said to have formed the basis of Asian civilisation, turning **nomadic** hunter-gatherers into land-cultivating farmers. It created a revolution in societal organisation, leading to the development of the first densely populated urban centres.

c It was first cultivated high in the Andes on the shores of Lake Titicaca, between 3000 and 7000 years ago. Wild plants grew around the lake and Inca farmers began cultivating them as they are easy to grow and are also high in nutrients.

d It became a staple crop throughout Central America and helped to **sustain** the great cities of the Incan empire. The Incas preserved it by dehydrating and mashing it so that any food surplus could be stored for up to ten years.

e At the beginning of the 16th century, Portuguese traders seeking **lucrative** trade routes arrived in Sri Lanka where this crop was grown. They took control of the area and started their own monopoly, which lasted for 100 years.

f In 17th-century Japan, it was at the centre of the economy. Different parts of the country were ranked according to their harvesting capacity. It was collected as a tax from farmers by the rulers of each region and turned into money.

g Because it requires highly organised labour as well as sophisticated management of land and water, it is thought that this crop may have helped create more cooperative and **tight-knit** communities as well as unique cultural rituals.

6 What it is to be human

h In the 17th century, the Dutch took control of the island and also of the monopoly. However, when it was discovered that this crop could be easily grown in other places, the value of the trade declined. ☐

i Spanish sailors brought the plants to Europe in the 16th century, where they soon became a popular agricultural crop. By the 18th century, many countries included it as part of their diet. However, a **blight** in the 1840s resulted in severe crop losses, hunger and starvation for communities such as Irish farmers, who relied on it as their main source of food. ☐

3 Which food descriptions from Exercise 2 contain information about the following? Write the food name(s).

  a geopolitical competition ....

  b economic expansion ....

  c social transformation ....

4 Match the words in bold from the descriptions in Exercise 2 with the correct meanings below.

  a wandering from one place to another ....

  b profitable ....

  c connected to the sea ....

  d disease or plague ....

  e feed and support ....

  f closely connected ....

Challenge

5 Find out about one of the foods in the box below and its role in history. Write a summary in your notebook, of around 150 words.

| tea | bread | salt | sugar |

Use of English: Modal verbs for speculating and making deductions

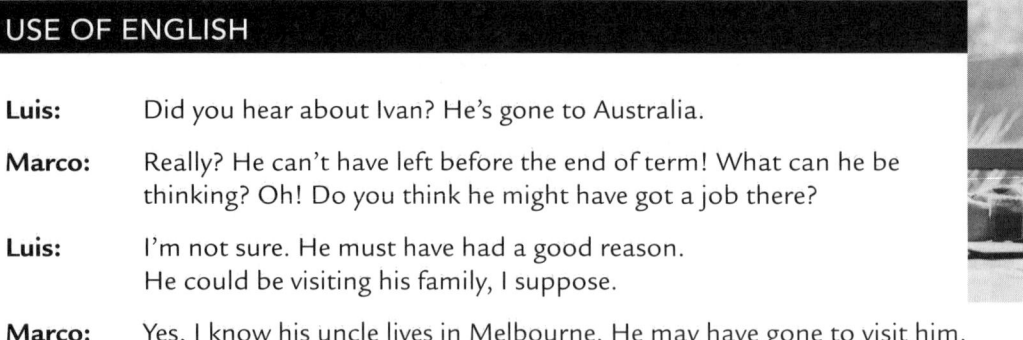

USE OF ENGLISH

Luis: Did you hear about Ivan? He's gone to Australia.

Marco: Really? He can't have left before the end of term! What can he be thinking? Oh! Do you think he might have got a job there?

Luis: I'm not sure. He must have had a good reason.
He could be visiting his family, I suppose.

Marco: Yes, I know his uncle lives in Melbourne. He may have gone to visit him.

Luis: That sounds more likely. He must be coming back to school after the vacation.

Check!

1 Read the conversation above between two students.
Underline the modal verbs of speculation and deduction.

Notice

2 Which modal verbs express certainty? Which are more uncertain?

....

....

Focus

3 **Rewrite the underlined sentences using the modal verbs provided.**

a The music is very loud. They are having a party. (must)

....

b George isn't at school today. He probably caught a cold. (might)

....

c You've just eaten lunch. You aren't hungry again already? (can't)

....

d Yasmin isn't answering her phone. Maybe she didn't take her phone today. (might)

....

e There are a lot of letters on their front doorstep. Have they gone on holiday? (could)

....

Practice

4 **Which sentences contain modal verbs that can be replaced with *can*? Circle the verbs.**

a I've lost my keys. They could be on my desk at school.

b Not drinking enough water could make you feel tired.

c I think they might have missed the train.

d The match could be cancelled tomorrow because of rain.

e Extra traffic may cause delays at the airport.

Challenge

5 **Write two sentences for each of the following situations, using modal verbs of speculation or deduction.**

a He's looking around his back garden at night with a torch.

....

....

b Their car has been parked outside their house all day.

....

....

c She sold her house and bought a new car.

....

....

> **GET IT RIGHT!**
>
> We do not usually use *can* when speaking about probability but instead use *could*, *may* or *might*. *Can* is used to talk about more general possibilities.
>
> Examples:
> *Why is Jane absent today? She **could** have a cold.* (probability)
>
> *It **can** get very cold in the winter.* (general possibility)

Use of English: Passive voice

USE OF ENGLISH

The conformity experiment

In the 1950s, an experiment was conducted to find out whether people can be made to change their beliefs by the pressure to conform. In this experiment, a student was introduced to a group of 6–8 other students. They were actors who had already been told the true purpose of the experiment. The group was shown two cards with lines on them, and was asked to say which lines matched. When incorrect answers were given by all the actors in the group, the subjects also gave the incorrect answer, despite being given clear visual evidence that it was wrong.

Check!

1 Read the description above of a psychology experiment. Underline uses of the passive voice.

Notice

2 Which of these statements about the passive are true? Tick the correct answers.

We can use the passive…

A if the agent is unknown or unimportant ☐

B to look at an action from the point of view of the person affected by it ☐

C in past, present or future forms ☐

D with modals ☐

E in gerund or infinitive forms ☐

F with intransitive verbs ☐

Focus

3 Complete these sentences using the passive form of the verbs given.

a Conformity .... (can, define) as the tendency for people to change their beliefs to match the social group around them.

b After .... (show) two cards with lines on them, the subjects selected the lines that were the same length.

c The subjects of the experiment were not aware that the other students

.... (tell) to give incorrect answers.

d   Afterwards, some of the subjects said that they gave incorrect answers because they did not want .... (ridicule) by the others.

e   Some subjects said they believed that the others .... (may, better inform) than they were.

> **GET IT RIGHT!**
>
> Remember to use the correct form of *be* or *have* and the past participle when forming the passive.
>
> Examples:
> They **had been** given special instructions before the test. (not *had be*)
>
> The article **was written** by several psychology professors. (not *wrote*)

Practice

4 Find and correct the errors. One sentence is correct.

a   The subjects may have influenced by several factors.

b   Afterwards, they were explained the real purpose of the experiment.

c   They would have changed their selection, if they were not in a group.

d   It showed that peer pressure can persuade people to change their beliefs.

e   The experiment has been repeat several times with similar results.

f   The results of the experiments published in an academic journal.

Challenge

5 Complete the description with verbs in the active or passive form.

The invisible gorilla experiment

This study ....¹ (conduct) in 1999 at Harvard University. Participants ....² (ask) to watch a video in which six players play basketball. They ....³ (instruct) to count how many passes occurred between players on one of the teams. Most participants ....⁴ (complete) the task without any difficulty. However, in the middle of the video, a man wearing a gorilla suit walked into the picture. Instead of ....⁵ (distract) by the gorilla, most people just ....⁶ (ignore) it. It ....⁷ (find) that half of the people who watched the video ....⁸ (miss) the gorilla completely.

Academic writing: Summarising

1 Complete the tips for writing a good summary.

A good summary starts by introducing the ....[1] idea. It should be written in your own ....[2]. It is important to include all the ....[3] ideas and only include minor ....[4] if they are necessary. You do not need to include your own ....[5] or interpretation in a summary. It's a good idea to conclude by ....[6] the main idea.

2 Number these steps in the best order for writing a summary.

a Identify the supporting arguments. ☐
b Read and revise your draft. ☐
c Identify the main points. ☐
d Read the article carefully. ☐
e Write your first draft. ☐

3 You are going to write a summary of this article. First, skim the article and underline the main ideas.

How we judge personality from faces depends on our pre-existing beliefs about how personality work

We make **snap judgements** of others based not only on their facial appearance, but also on our pre-existing beliefs about how others' personalities work, finds a new study by a team of psychology researchers.

Its work, reported in the journal *Proceedings of the National Academy of Sciences*, **underscores** how we interpret others' facial features to form impressions of their personalities.

'People form personality impressions from others' facial appearance within only a few hundred milliseconds,' observes Jonathan Freeman, the paper's senior author and an associate professor in New York University's Department of Psychology and Center for **Neural** Science. 'Our findings suggest that face impressions are shaped not only by a face's specific features but also by our own beliefs about personality – for instance, the **cues** that make a face look competent and make a face look friendly are physically more similar for those who believe competence and friendliness co-occur in other people's personalities.'

'Although these impressions are highly **reliable**, they are often quite inaccurate,' Freeman adds. 'And yet they are consequential, as previous research has found face impressions to predict a range of real-world outcomes, from political elections, to hiring decisions or criminal sentencing. Initial impressions of faces can bias how we interact and make critical decisions about people, and so understanding the mechanisms behind these impressions is important for developing techniques to reduce biases based on facial features that typically operate outside of awareness.'

snap judgements: judgements we make instantly, without carefully considering them

underscores: emphasises the importance of something

neural: relating to the nerves or the nervous system, including the brain

cues: actions that are signals for something

reliable: (in statistics) consistent, when the same results occur every time

4 Read these statements. Number them in the best order for a summary. Write X if the statement is inaccurate or is not a main idea.

a Facial cues for friendliness are quite different from those for competence.

b For example, we may believe that friendliness and competence frequently co-occur.

c Judgements based on appearance can play an important role in many contexts.

d People aren't usually aware of any bias they have towards others based on their facial appearance.

e The article discusses how we form judgements about other people when we first meet them.

f It suggests that our judgements are based not only on visual information, but also on our beliefs about personality.

g Therefore, we are more likely to think that friendly-looking people are competent.

h In conclusion, the results of this study reveal the close links between pre-existing beliefs and personality judgements.

i Understanding how this works is important to reducing bias in critical situations.

Challenge

5 **Choose one of the experiments described in the previous lesson on the passive voice. Write a summary of the experiment in your notebook using 50 words or less.**

Check your progress

Vocabulary

1 Complete the puzzle using the clues below. What is the mystery word?

1. period of time before written records
2. pathways from one place to another
3. relating to the sea or the ocean
4. a basic or fundamental food or crop
5. advantages
6. a nutrient found in meat, fish and dairy products
7. harmful or damaging
8. the way in which you live

Mystery word: ………………………..

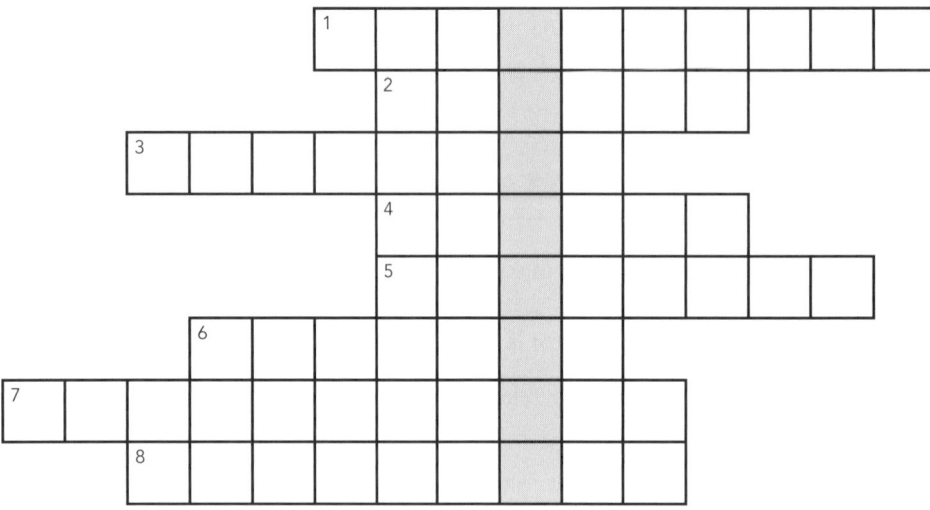

Grammar

2 Circle the best words to complete the sentences.

a Elena missed her lessons today. She *might / must / can't* have gone to the dentist.

b These photos are amazing. You *could / can / must* be a professional photographer one day.

c Karel passed the exam with top marks. He *must / can't / could* have studied really hard.

d You *can't / could / must* have seen me in the café. I was in the library all day.

3 Complete the sentences using the passive form of the verbs provided.

Blue zones

A team of researchers investigated countries where people frequently live to be centenarians. These places ....¹ (know) as the Blue Zones. It ....² (discover) that certain lifestyle characteristics ....³ (share) by people in all five zones. One factor was eating a mainly plant-based diet. Meat ....⁴ (eat) only about five times a month. Regular exercise ....⁵ (include) as a natural part of their daily routine and people ....⁶ (encourage) to stay healthy and happy by a strong social network. The study concluded that longevity doesn't improve when people ....⁷ (tell) to diet and exercise. It ....⁸ (can, do) more effectively by making small social and environmental changes instead.

Reading

4 Read the paragraph and answer the questions.

Emotional intelligence

We often think of emotions as a distraction from rational judgements and decision-making, but emotions are actually a fundamental part of our social interactions. Emotional intelligence is a term used to describe our ability to recognise and manage our own emotions and those of other people. **This** is especially important for people in positions of leadership and helps them to make effective decisions.

a Summarise the main idea of the paragraph in one sentence.

   ....

b What does the word *This* in line 8 refer to?

   ....

c Give one example of a situation where emotional intelligence might help you.

   ....

Writing

5 Choose a reading passage from Units 1–5 of Coursebook 11 or this Workbook. Write a summary of the passage in your notebook, using 100 words or less.

REFLECTION

Write answers to these questions in your notebook.

a Choose five interesting words from this unit and draw pictures to go with them in your notebook. How did visualisation help you to remember them?

b How has your view of how food influences history changed because of what you have learnt in this unit? What kinds of food do you think influence society today?

c What do you think are the most important traits of being human? Name two ways in which you have developed your understanding of the word *humanity*.

d Look back at your last essay and find three places where you could have used the passive voice.

e What did you learn about writing a summary? In what situations would summarising be useful as an academic study skill?

7 Tiny wonders

Think about it: The magic of microscopic marine organisms

1 Complete the paragraph using words from the box.

> atmosphere   biological carbon pump   carbon dioxide   ecosystem   food web
> microorganisms   microplastics   photosynthesis   phytoplankton   pollutants

The word ....¹ is derived from the Greek words **phyto** (plant) and **plankton** (to wander or drift). They are single-cell ....² that live just beneath the water's surface and are an important part of the marine ....³. Phytoplankton have chlorophyll – just like land plants – which can capture sunlight and turn it into energy. Through the process of ....⁴, they absorb carbon dioxide and release oxygen. Phytoplankton are the foundation of the aquatic ....⁵ as they provide food for many small sea creatures, which are then eaten by larger fish and sea mammals. They transfer about ten gigatonnes of ....⁶ from the ....⁷ to the deep ocean each year. This is known as the ....⁸. Phytoplankton are endangered by ....⁹ such as factory waste and by ....¹⁰, which break up into small pieces and do not decompose.

2 Are these statements true (T) or false (F)? Circle the correct answer.
Correct the false statements.

a   Phytoplankton live on the ocean floor.   T   F

b   They convert oxygen and sunlight into energy.   T   F

c   They are eaten by fish and other creatures.   T   F

d   They can help reduce global warming.   T   F

e   They help reduce microplastics in the ocean.   T   F

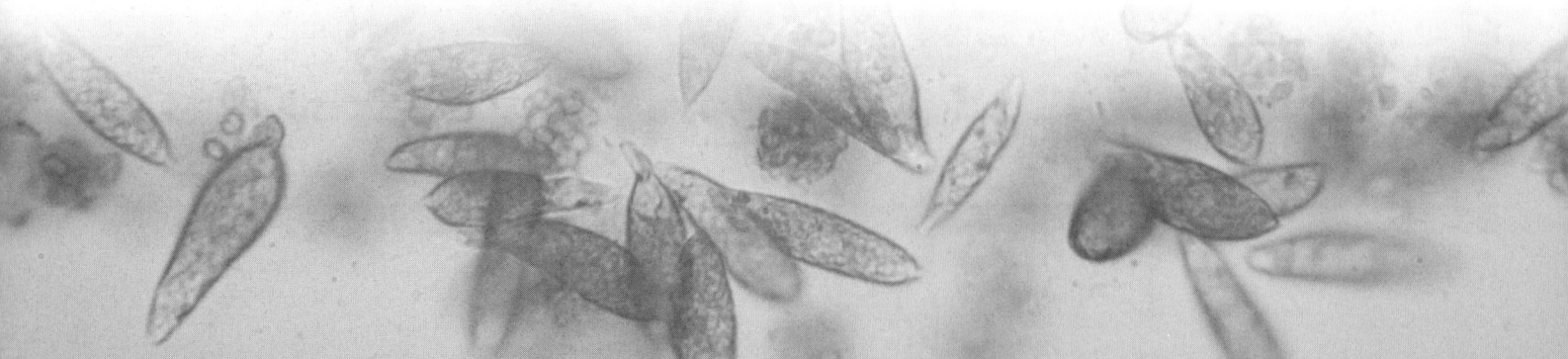

7 Tiny wonders

3   Read the information, then answer the questions.

Phytoplankton blooms

Under certain environmental conditions phytoplankton can reproduce rapidly, resulting in a huge, dense cloud known as a bloom. These blooms are clearly visible and can cover hundreds of square kilometres, causing the water to appear blue, green, brown or red depending on the pigment of the organism.

A bloom takes place if certain factors are favourable. First, the water temperature and salinity have to be at a certain level. Secondly, certain nutrients in the water have to be readily available. Phytoplankton absorb nutrients, mainly nitrogen and phosphorus, directly from the surrounding water. If these nutrients reach a certain concentration, a bloom can occur.

One example of a bloom happens when plant fertilisers containing nitrogen and phosphorus pour into coastal waters after heavy rainfall. In such cases, the bloom grows rapidly but then quickly disperses. If the favourable conditions persist, blooms may become more permanent, which can negatively impact the ecosystem. They may block the sunlight reaching seagrass on the ocean bed, which can stress or kill the plants.

a   What is a phytoplankton bloom?

   ....

b   What factors influence the occurrence of a bloom?

   ....

c   Why can heavy rainfall cause a bloom?

   ....

d   Why can plants on the ocean bed be negatively affected?

   ....

4   Find the words in the text with these meanings.

   a   describing something that can be seen   ....

   b   something that causes colour   ....

   c   the amount of salt in water   ....

   d   to continue for a period of time   ....

Challenge

5   **Find out three more interesting facts about phytoplankton. Summarise the information in your notebook.**

Biology: Tiny creatures

1 Look at the pictures on these pages. Write three facts you know about bees.

....

....

....

2 Read the article and find out whether your facts are mentioned.

Tiny pollinators

1. Next time you take a bite of a juicy apple or a peach, spare a moment to think about a tiny creature that plays a big role in creating your delicious fruit. Many of the fruits and other crops that we eat – from apples and blueberries to cabbages and pumpkins – rely on bees to pollinate them so they can produce fruit.

2. Bees visit a wide variety of flowering plants to gather pollen and nectar and take them back as food for their hive. Bees are uniquely designed to be excellent pollinators. They have hairs all over their body, which attract pollen. They also use hairs on their legs to comb the pollen into special pockets on their bodies. When the bee moves on, some of the pollen transfers to the next flower, allowing it to fertilise and become a seed.

3. Some predators, such as bears and skunks, sometimes destroy beehives to get at their honey. But the main dangers that bees face are caused by humans. The use of pesticides, intended to eradicate harmful insects, kills bees as well. As bees sometimes travel for kilometres in search of food, spraying just one crop can affect hundreds of hives.

4. Another danger for bees is climate change. As a result of global warming, flowers may bloom and produce pollen earlier in spring, before bees are ready to start feeding. This can severely impact bees' health, making them less likely to reproduce and more susceptible to illness.

5. Increased human population is also causing deforestation and destruction of shrubland, which are bees' natural habitats and feeding grounds. Most bees feed on a wide variety of plants, but some species only feed on one or two types of plants, and if they become scarce, they will be unable to feed.

6. Bee population numbers have fallen significantly in the last few years, and although they are not in danger of extinction, if this trend continues there may be severe implications not only for bees but also for the plants they pollinate – and for our ecosystem as a whole. To ensure their survival, it is vital that we take steps to create habitats that are pesticide-free and provide ample sources of nectar and pollen, as well as places for bees to build their hives.

3   Which paragraph in the article mentions the following?

   a   physical adaptations of bees ☐

   b   the interdependence of the ecosystem ☐

   c   some advice on how to protect bees ☐

   d   how farming practices affect bees ☐

   e   why biodiversity is important ☐

4   Find words in the article that match these meanings.

   a   vulnerable   ....

   b   destroy or kill ....

   c   gathering   ....

   d   difficult to find ....

5   Summarise the main idea of the article in one sentence.

   ....

Challenge

6   Research other pollinators that are important to our ecosystem. Choose one and find three interesting facts about it. Write them in your notebook and share them with the class in your next lesson.

Use of English: Prefixes in scientific language

USE OF ENGLISH

Coral reefs

Coral reefs are home to a fascinating and biodiverse marine environment. Although they are sometimes mistaken for rocks, corals are actually invertebrate animals. Coral reefs are made up of thousands of microorganisms called polyps, which create an exoskeleton that attaches to submerged rocks. Corals live in an interdependent relationship with a type of algae called zooxanthellae, which provide coral with food through photosynthesis. They also give coral its magnificent colours. When coral becomes stressed by changes in hydrodynamic conditions, it can start to expel these cells, leading to discolouration or bleaching.

Check!

1 Read the description. Underline ten words that use prefixes.

2 Match the underlined words with the meaning of their prefix.

    a between ....

    b connected with living creatures ....

    c below ....

    d wrongly ....

    e outer/outside of ....

    f not ....

    g small ....

    h water ....

    i light ....

    j opposite of ....

Notice

3 Which of the prefixes in Exercise 2 negate the meaning of the root word? Which prefixes add extra meaning to the root?

    Negate the meaning: ....

    Add extra meaning: ....

Focus

4 Match the definitions with words from the description of coral reefs.

    a a very tiny creature ....

    b to lose colour ....

    c to be under water ....

    d to convert sunlight into oxygen ....

    e without a spine ....

    f movement of water ....

Practice

5 Complete these sentences with adjectives using words from the box and the prefix *in-* or its variations.

accurate   logic   measure   partial   reverse

a This scanner keeps giving us different results.
   It's completely ....

b The report is not organised in a rational way. It is ....

c Once fossil fuels have been burnt, they cannot be replaced.
   The process is ....

d Objectivity is essential – you have to be totally ....

e The effects of ocean acidification are difficult to calculate and are probably ....

Challenge

6 Complete the paragraph with roots from the box and a prefix from Exercise 1.

classified   filtration   mobile   possible   tidal

Barnacles

Once ....[1] as a type of mollusc, barnacles are actually a type of crustacean. They have a flat, round shell that sticks to surfaces using a glue-like substance which is virtually ....[2] to remove. Once attached, they are completely ....[3]. They prefer shallow water with lots of activity such as ....[4] zones. Barnacles play an important role in ....[5] as they clean dissolved debris from the water.

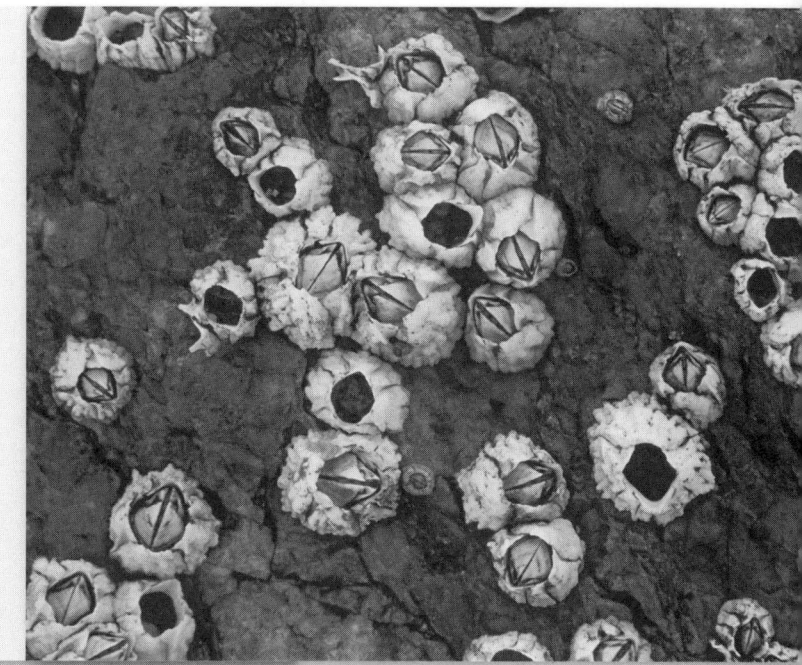

> **GET IT RIGHT!**
>
> *In-* is a prefix that gives a word its opposite meaning. There are variations of *in-* depending on the first letter of the root word. Use *im-* (before m, b or p), *il-* (before l) and *ir-* (before r).
>
> Examples:
> *im*possible
> *il*legal
> *ir*responsible
>
> Note that not all words starting with these letters use variations of *in-*.
>
> Examples:
> *un*believable
> *un*lawful
> *un*reliable

Use of English: Adverbs for report writing

USE OF ENGLISH

Check!

1 Read the report. Underline the adverbs of certainty, manner or degree.

Water-quality report

It was found that nitrate levels at several beaches had risen dramatically, resulting in frequent algae blooms that negatively impact marine life. Water samples were taken regularly over a period of six months from collection points that were deliberately chosen to represent a wide range of tidal activity. The results consistently showed that before heavy rainfall, nitrate levels were relatively low compared with afterwards, when levels rose significantly. We consider it highly probable that fertiliser run-off from surrounding farms has contributed to this increase. We therefore conclude that rerouting run-off through canals and reservoirs would undoubtedly limit fluctuations in nitrate levels and the frequency of algae blooms could possibly be reduced as a result.

Notice

2 Which of the words that you underlined in the report are…

a adverbs of certainty? ....

b adverbs of manner? ....

c adverbs of degree? ....

Focus

3 Which of the adverbs in the report could be replaced with the words below?

a carefully ....
b certainly ....
c extremely ....
d fairly ....
e greatly ....
f probably ....
g reliably ....
h repeatedly ....
i considerably ....
j unfavourably ....

Practice

4 Draw a caret (^) to show where the adverb (in brackets) could be placed in each sentence. There may be more than one possibility.

a We will examine the evidence. (carefully)

b They didn't understand the instructions. (correctly)

c The local transport system has improved. (considerably)

d The numbers of bees and butterflies have increased. (greatly)

e The study revealed that pollution levels were low. (relatively)

Challenge

5 Complete the description using adverb forms of the words in the box.

| close   clear   complete   consider   doubt |
| extreme   potential   responsible |

Plastic-eating enzymes

Recent research suggests that microbes in oceans and soils could ....[1] have the ability to eat plastic. It is vital to try to dispose of the plastic ....[2] without harming the environment, but many types of plastic do not degrade ....[3] and are ....[4] hard to recycle. Using enzymes to break down plastics could ....[5] speed up the recycling process. Recent studies have found that the number of enzymes is ....[6] higher than first thought. The next phase would be to examine these enzymes ....[7] under laboratory conditions and learn more about how they have evolved. According to this study, enzymes will ....[8] have an important role to play in saving our planet.

> **GET IT RIGHT!**
>
> Adverbs usually go between an auxiliary and the main verb.
>
> Example:
> *The report didn't **significantly** change our opinion.*
>
> Adverbs of manner and degree can also go after the object.
>
> Example:
> *The report didn't change our opinion **significantly**.*
>
> When using adverbs with an adjective, put the adverb before the adjective.
>
> Example:
> *The report showed **significantly** higher levels of air pollution.*

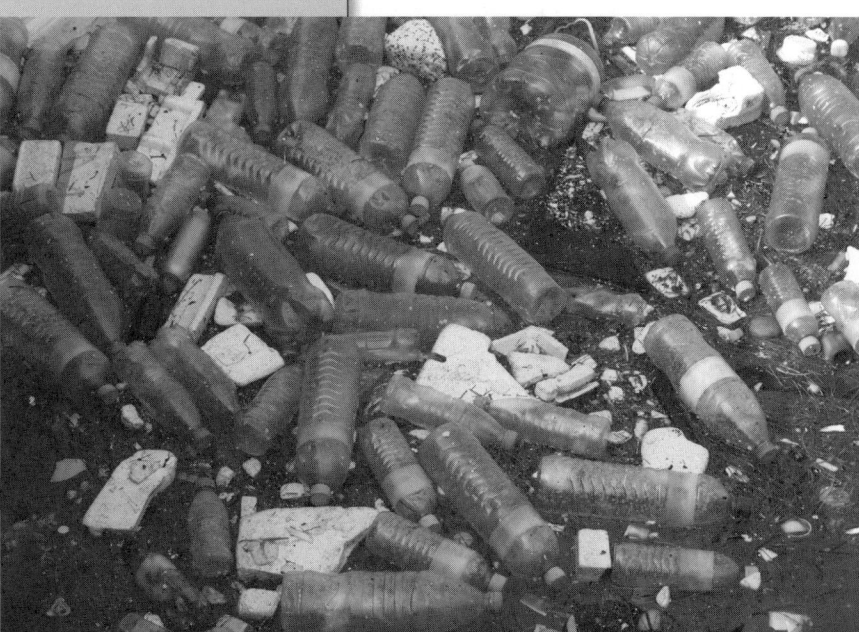

Academic writing: A report

1 Read the title of the report. Write three questions that you think the report might answer.

....

....

....

2 Read the report. Which of your questions were answered?

Microplastics in drinking water

Abstract

This report presents the results of a study of the presence of microplastics in our drinking water. It investigates the concentrations of microplastics and their probable source.

Introduction

Microplastics have been detected in a broad range of water-based environments, including marine water, waste water, fresh water and drinking water. There is increasing concern about the potentially harmful effects they could have on human and marine life.

Background

Although plastics have been produced and used for a wide range of applications for decades, little is known about their process of degradation. It is generally accepted that plastics do not decompose but are broken up into smaller particles.

Method

Five hundred water samples were collected from both tap water and bottled water in 35 locations around the country. The concentration of particles in the water was evaluated. The particles were analysed to identify the probable source of their production.

Results

It was found that over 80% of all samples contained tiny plastic particles, with an average of 4.34 plastic particles per litre of water. The main categories of particles were microfibres (derived from synthetic textiles and released during machine washing) and degraded plastic waste (resulting from fragmentation of larger products).

Discussion

Current water treatment facilities focus on removing toxins and harmful chemicals, and are not designed to effectively remove microplastics. Therefore, they end up in the ocean and in rivers.

Recommendations

Our study indicates that as microplastics are so prevalent in our environment, it will be important to investigate their effect on the human body. It may also become important to explore the development of effective microplastic filtration methods in water-treatment facilities.

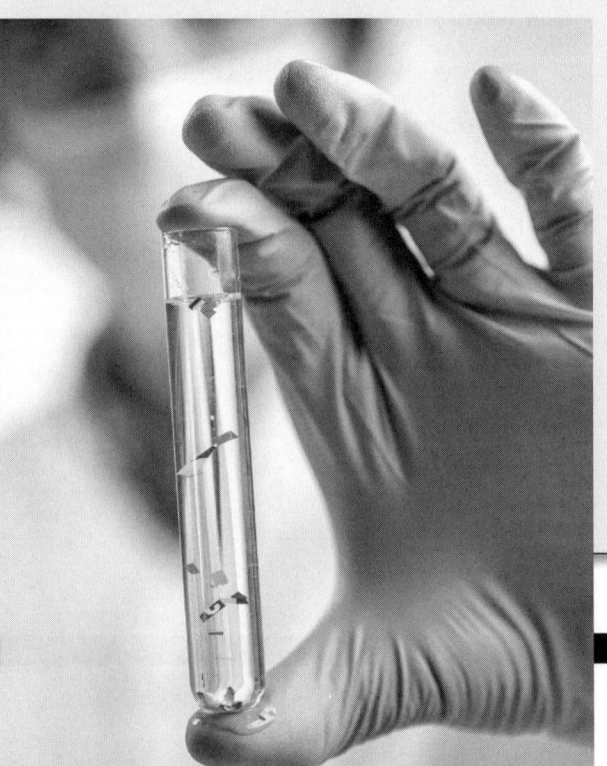

3 **These statements are missing from the report.**
For each statement, write the section of the report it belongs in.

a For the purposes of this study, a microplastic is defined as <5 mm in length.

....

b This research also suggests that reducing our consumption of plastic products and promoting the use of eco-friendly products would be a major step towards reducing the presence of microplastics in our drinking water.

....

c Microplastics are ingested by small marine creatures and gradually become part of the food chain, with potential implications for human health.

....

d The concentration of these particles will accumulate as more plastic is released into the environment. ....

e A large percentage of the particles detected were <1 mm in length.

....

f Therefore, it has become increasingly important to obtain reliable data on the extent of microparticles in our drinking water. ....

g It concludes with recommendations for further research. ....

4 **How reliable do you think this study is? What questions would you ask to verify its reliability? Write two ideas.**

....

....

5 **Survey your classmates or your family to find out how much plastic they throw away every day and how they dispose of it. Write a report in your notebook to describe your findings.**

Check your progress

Vocabulary

> bloom   crustacean   deforestation
> ecosystem   extinction   microbiology
> pollen   predators

1 Choose one of the words from the box to complete each sentence.

a Crabs and lobsters are two species of ....

b Owls, hawks and snakes eat bats, and are their main ....

c Bees feed on plants and fertilise them by transferring ....

d The black rhinoceros is in danger of ....

e Cutting down trees for farming contributes to global ....

f By filtering sea water, barnacles help to maintain their ....

g The study of very small creatures is known as ....

h When phytoplankton suddenly multiply, it is called a ....

Grammar

2 Write the words in the correct column using the appropriate prefix.

> appoint   available   communicate
> efficient   helpful   honest   match
> obedient   organic   understand
> usual   visible

in-	un-

dis-	mis-

3 Replace the words in bold with adverbs usually used for report writing. More than one answer may be possible.

a Water pollution levels increased **by a small amount**. ....

b Floods and storms **often** cause damage to the coastline. ....

c Improved filtration systems could **perhaps** prevent water contamination. ....

d The number of microparticles in the ocean increased **a lot**. ....

e The reduced traffic flow **certainly** had a positive effect on air pollution. ....

Reading

4 Find these words in the information about bumblebee bats below. Use the context to work out their meaning. Then write a synonym or a definition in your own words.

a insectivorous ....

b dusk and dawn ....

c echolocation ....

d prey ....

e roost ....

f colonies ....

> The bumblebee bat (*Craseonycteris thonglongyai*) is the smallest mammal in the world. It weighs less than two grams and its body reaches a length of 33 millimetres – the size of a large bumblebee, hence its name. They are insectivorous and fly only at dusk and dawn, when they search for food around bamboo clumps and teak trees using echolocation to find their prey. They like to roost deep inside limestone caves where they live in colonies of between 100 and 500 bats. These bats have so far been found only in the rainforests of Myanmar and in Thailand. They are extremely rare and are classified as Vulnerable on the IUCN Red List of Threatened Species.

5 Read the information about bumblebee bats again. Then answer these questions.

a What does the text imply about the bats' feeding habits?

....

b What do you think are the most significant dangers these bats might face?

....

c What do you think 'classified as Vulnerable' means in the context of the IUCN Red List of Threatened Species?

....

d Find out about the IUCN Red List. How many categories are there and which animals are most endangered in the world today?

....
....
....

Writing

6 Choose one of the following topics. Write a report and make recommendations. Remember to include different sections in your report.

> What kind of recycling facilities are available in your school? How could they be improved?

> How aware are people in your class or in your family of microplastics in drinking water? What steps (if any) do they take to reduce them?

REFLECTION

Write answers to these questions in your notebook.

a What are the three most interesting facts you have learnt about tiny creatures? Which tasks in this unit helped you to learn about science?

b How did the information in this unit change your understanding of science?

c How did you practise using critical thinking skills in this unit? Why is critical thinking important when reading or listening in an academic context?

d Look at your last essay and find three places where you could add adverbs of certainty, manner or degree. Why is it important to reread your essays carefully?

e In what way did you learn to improve your report writing? Why is it important to organise your report into different sections?

8 Sustainability

Think about it: What is sustainability?

1 What do these photos have in common? Write three ideas in your notebook.

2 Complete the quiz to check your knowledge about sustainability.

How much do you know about sustainability?

a You are planning a holiday abroad. Which type of transportation would generate the lowest carbon emissions?
○ plane ○ train ○ bus

b You want to buy some new clothing. Which of the following textiles has the least harmful impact on the environment?
○ cotton ○ linen ○ polyester

c You are planning a menu for dinner. Which food causes least damage to the environment in its production?
○ rice ○ soybeans ○ pulses

d You are going to buy a soft drink in a supermarket. Which drinks container is best for the environment?
○ aluminium can
○ PET plastic bottle
○ glass bottle

e You want to throw away some old batteries. What should you do with them?
○ put them in the recycling bin
○ bury them in the garden
○ take them to a recycling centre

f You are buying some food to cook for dinner. Which is kindest to the planet?
○ lamb ○ chicken ○ fish

g You want to buy a toy for a young relative. Which material causes the most carbon emissions?
○ wood ○ metal ○ plastic

h Which of the following actions would not save energy in your home?
○ unplugging all appliances when not in use
○ taking a shower instead of a bath
○ replacing light bulbs and batteries frequently

Now check your answers on the next page. What's your score? ___ / 8

8   Sustainability

3   Which of these criteria were used in the quiz to define sustainability? Do you agree
    with these criteria? What other criteria can you think of? Add two ideas.

    a   reduces carbon footprint ☐   e   is good for your health ☐
    b   uses fewer natural resources to produce ☐   f   can be recycled ☐
    c   protects wildlife and biodiversity ☐   g   has social and economic benefits ☐
    d   uses renewable energy ☐   h   is less harmful to the environment ☐

    ....
    ....

4   Write one idea for how to make each of the following areas of your life more sustainable.

    a   how you travel to school or in your free time
        ....

    b   what food you choose to eat at home or at school
        ....

    c   what clothes or games and devices you buy
        ....

    d   everyday routines at home or at school
        ....

Challenge

5   Choose one of the following topics and explain how it can help the environment.
    How difficult would it be to do these things? Write a paragraph in your notebook.

    • Switching to a plant-based diet
    • Using sustainable criteria to make decisions about what you buy
    • Buying locally sourced food and other products
    • Using public transport instead of driving a car

---

a   Trains carry the most people and so have the lowest carbon emissions per passenger.
b   Linen (organic if possible) uses less water and fewer pesticides than cotton. Polyester is manufactured using fossil fuels and sheds microparticles when it is washed.
c   Pulses use less water and fewer pesticides and also produce more food per square metre.
d   Aluminium cans are easiest to recycle, although a lot of resources are used to manufacture them. Glass can also be recycled, but uses more fuel to transport.
e   Batteries contain toxic chemicals and should be taken to a recycling centre.
f   Fish is a good choice, as long as it is caught or farmed sustainably. Chicken is a better choice than other types of meat as it requires less land, food and water.
g   Wood does not produce carbon emissions in its manufacture and also traps carbon during its lifetime.
h   Replacing light bulbs and batteries doesn't save energy (unless you replace them with more energy-efficient models).

Business and environmental management: Embracing sustainability

1 Read the title of the article below. What kind of ideas do you expect to read about? Write three ideas.

....

....

....

How to go green in the office

Do you want to minimise your carbon footprint, but are worried that doing so might impact productivity? Think again! Creating a more sustainable workplace may not be as difficult as you might think. Even small changes can have a big impact. Here are some green ideas for the office that every company should use!

Paper

You probably already have paper recycling bins in your office, but have you thought about ways to reduce the amount of paper that goes into them? Add this line to the bottom of every email: *Do not print this email unless absolutely essential*. Avoid paper handouts at meetings. Send a pre- and post-meeting summary by email instead. Encourage all employees to print double-sided. This will automatically cut in half the amount of paper you use. For essential printing, supply 100% recycled paper.

Energy use

Turn off and unplug computers when you leave work. Turn off computers and lights in any rooms that are not being used. It can be helpful to install **motion-activated** light switches. Reducing your computer monitor **brightness** can save energy – and most people don't notice any difference! Finally, make sure that energy-saving mode is enabled on all monitors.

Single-use plastics

Reduce the number of plastic cups that are thrown away by providing reusable mugs with the company logo. If there is a kitchen area, provide reusable or compostable plates and **cutlery**. Similarly, work with your cafeteria or corporate hospitality manager to find suppliers that provide green alternatives. Consider a complete office-wide ban on single-use plastic cups.

Travel

Encourage employees to carpool by setting up a group booking app where people can offer to share their rides to work or home. Partner with nearby companies to provide more carpool opportunities. Provide incentives for not travelling by plane. How about an extra day's holiday for people who choose to travel by train instead? Encourage working from home at least one day a week, which will also help reduce your carbon footprint. For essential company travel, partner with a carbon reduction project to offset company emissions.

---

motion-activated: describing things that switch on when they detect movement

brightness: the amount of light something gives off

cutlery: knives, forks and spoons

8 Sustainability

2 **Answer these questions about the article.**

   a Who do you think is the intended audience for this article?

      ....

   b Which of the ideas in the article do you think…

      i would be easiest to implement?

         ....

      ii would be most difficult to implement?

         ....

      iii employees might object to and why?

         ....

3 **Find words in the article with these meanings.**

   a reduce or make smaller   ....

   b the rate at which work gets done   ....

   c relating to a business or company   ....

   d decays or disintegrates after time   ....

   e something that motivates you   ....

   f join with or collaborate   ....

4 **How could the following changes help to reduce carbon emissions?**

   a using recycled paper

      ....

   b motion-activated light switches

      ....

   c carpool booking app

      ....

   d offsetting carbon emissions

      ....

Challenge

5 **Think of three ways to reduce the carbon footprint at your school. In your notebook, write an email to your classmates outlining your suggestions and persuading them to take part.**

Use of English: Syntax – premodifying noun phrases

USE OF ENGLISH

What is responsible travel?

Responsible travel refers to the behaviour of travellers who make choices according to sustainable tourism principles. This need not be a complicated time-consuming process. Many online travel agencies now link to environmentally friendly tour operators that hold an official sustainability certification. However, there are different certification schemes around the world, each of which has its own specific evaluative criteria. Some of the more widely trusted programmes assess energy efficiency, water conservation and waste reduction. Others also include factors such as energy from renewable carbon-free sources and locally sourced organic food.

Check!

1 Read the description above. Underline nouns that have at least two premodifying words.

2 Write the noun phrases from Exercise 1 in the correct place in the table.

adjective + noun + head noun	
	....
	....
	....
adjective + adjective + head noun	
	....
	....
adverb + adjective + head noun	
	....
	....
	....

Notice

3 Which of the premodifiers from the table in Exercise 2 are participles?

....

Focus

4 Rewrite the underlined phrases using premodified noun phrases.

a This is a certification that is recognised internationally.

....

b More travellers are choosing hotels that have been approved by official sources.

....

c We use criteria for sustainability that are researched carefully.

....

d Hotels are given a rating on how eco-friendly they are, based on their performance.

....

e We implement a system of management that is sensitive to the environment.

....

Practice

5 Complete the sentences with the -ed or -ing participle form of verbs in the box.

~~break~~ power craft provoke save speak

Example: *We finished the race in record-**breaking** time.*

a The gift shop offers a range of hand-............................ ceramics and pottery.

b The tour company has a useful time-............................ app for planning your trip.

c The hotel uses wind-............................ generators for all its energy needs.

d It's good to visit an English-............................ country in order to practise the language.

e The tour guide gave us a very thought-............................ account of the museum's history.

Challenge

6 Write a short description of your ideal eco-friendly resort in your notebook. Use as many of the words in the box as you can.

| community based   environmentally friendly   high quality |
internationally recognised   locally sourced   sustainably managed

LANGUAGE TIP

Compound adjectives that use a noun and a participle usually have a hyphen.

Examples:
*The restaurant menu had many **plant-based** options.*

*The employees participate in the **decision-making** process.*

Note that not all compound adjectives with participles are hyphenated.

Examples:
homemade, mouthwatering, breathtaking

Use of English: Linking and transition words

USE OF ENGLISH

Why is sustainability education important?

What better place is there to start building habits for a sustainable lifestyle than at school? School is where children learn about the world around them. Furthermore, they acquire the values that will guide them throughout the rest of their lives. Therefore, it is crucial to teach children the skills to understand environmental issues. For instance, they can learn how to reduce waste and increase their use of renewable and recyclable resources. In conclusion, sustainability education can have a significant impact on protecting our planet for future generations.

Check!

1 Read the article above. Underline the linking words and phrases.

Notice

2 What do the linking words and phrases have in common concerning their position in the sentence and their punctuation?

....

....

3 Which of the linking words in the article can be replaced with the following?

a as a result/consequently ....
c in addition/moreover ....

b in summary/to sum up ....
d for example ....

Focus

4 **Circle the correct linking word to complete these sentences.**

a Sustainability affects social, environmental and economic aspects of our lives.

Therefore, / Furthermore, sustainability education should integrate topics from all subject areas.

b Changing behaviour now will benefit the wellbeing of future generations.

In conclusion, / In addition, sustainability is an essential element of every education programme.

c One way to develop these skills is to identify problems in their school.

For example, / Consequently, they can identify ways to increase recycling.

Practice

5 **Rewrite the information using linking words from Exercises 1 or 3.**

a   There are many ways to reduce energy usage.
    You can walk to school or ride a bike.

    ....

b   Fast fashion encourages us to buy new clothes frequently.
    We frequently throw clothes away.

    ....

c   Organic farming reduces harmful substances, conserves water and increases soil fertility. It has many benefits for our environment.

    ....

d   Buying locally produced food cuts down on fuel used for transportation. You can avoid buying food that is wrapped in plastic.

    ....

GET IT RIGHT!

Linking and transition words are often used at the start of a sentence and are followed by a comma. Unlike connectives such as *so* and *because*, they are *not* used to join two clauses.

Examples:
Sea levels are predicted to rise. Consequently, many communities will be flooded. (not ..., consequently many communities will be flooded)

Challenge

6 **Complete the description below using linking words from the box. More than one answer may be possible in some of the gaps.**

> although   as well as   because   but   consequently
> for example   furthermore   in addition   instead of
> moreover   so   therefore   to sum up

Sustainable shopping

There are many ways to think about sustainability when you are shopping. Every product you buy has an environmental impact when it is produced. ....¹, it can harm the environment when it is thrown away. ....², it is important to choose products with a low carbon footprint. Read labels carefully.

..........................³, when you buy tea or coffee, buy brands that are grown sustainably ....⁴ and don't destroy rainforests. Clothing can cause pollution ....⁵ it uses a lot of pesticides and fossil fuels in its production ....⁶ toxic chemical dyes. Therefore, ...⁷ buying new clothes, consider buying vintage or second-hand. ....⁸, just a few simple changes in your lifestyle can have a big impact on reducing your carbon footprint.

Academic writing: Expository essay

1 There are several ways to write a 'hook' to start your essay.
   Read the task, then draw lines to match the examples with the type of hook.

   Describe how deforestation is affecting our planet.

   a Trees absorb greenhouse gases that cause climate change.   an eye-catching statement

   b Two thousand four hundred trees are cut down each minute.   a surprising statistic

   c How do trees save us from global warming?   a quotation

   d 'By destroying the animals, the air, and the trees,   a general truth
      we are destroying ourselves.' Thích Nhất Hạnh
                                                                         a question
   e Deforestation is rapidly devastating our planet.

2 The next sentence should give some background to the topic.
   Tick the best sentence to continue the paragraph.

   A Forests provide a vital habitat for hundreds of wildlife species. ☐
   B Trees remove air pollution by absorbing carbon dioxide.   ☐
   C Whenever trees are cut down, they should be replaced.   ☐

3 The final sentence is your thesis statement.
   Choose the best thesis statement for this essay.

   A The best way to stop deforestation is to create protected areas
      of rainforest that no one is allowed to cut down.   ☐
   B Rainforests have a vital role in the ecology of our planet, and
      there are several ways in which widespread deforestation is having
      a negative impact.   ☐
   C Deforestation is the process by which much of the world's forests are
      being cut down, yet there are many ways in which this could be reversed. ☐

4 Write the introductory paragraph to the essay in your notebook.

> **WRITING TIP**
>
> An expository essay presents information about a topic. Examples of expository essay writing include presenting a description or a definition, comparing and contrasting, explaining cause and effect, and describing a problem and a solution. The purpose of an expository essay is to explain or describe something and to explore aspects of the topic in more detail. It is not necessary to give your opinion. The tone should be neutral and objective.

5 Complete the outline with ideas for your essay.
Then write the essay in your notebook.

| Introductory paragraph |
| .... |
| .... |

↓

| Body paragraph 1 |
| .... |
| .... |

↓

| Body paragraph 2 |
| .... |
| .... |

↓

| Body paragraph 3 |
| .... |
| .... |

↓

| Conclusion |
| .... |
| .... |

6 Read your essay aloud. Identify places where you could make your language more concise by using premodified noun phrases.

Check your progress

Vocabulary

1 Replace the words and phrases in bold with appropriate words and phrases from this unit. Write the answers in your notebook.

To:	All employees
From:	Management

We're excited to tell you about our new initiative to make our company more **environmentally responsible**[1]. Our aim is to **reduce**[2] the carbon **emissions**[3] generated by our company. We plan to use energy sources that are **not based on fossil fuels**[4]. We also aim to **collaborate**[5] with other companies on eco-friendly projects. We spoke with our **social events**[6] manager about reducing single-use plastics, and we agreed only to use products that **can break down completely into harmless material**[7]. We also suggested providing food and beverages in our cafeteria that are **produced in our region**[8]. This green approach will become an important part of our **wider company**[9] identity and will have no impact on our **rate of work**[10]. We encourage everyone to take part in this fantastic initiative.

Grammar

2 Circle the correct words to complete the sentences.

a The energy plan is based on *total / totally* renewable resources.

b Our goal is to achieve carbon-zero *sustainability / sustainable* status by 2030.

c We encourage an imaginative problem-*solved / solving* approach to this project.

d The project is designed to protect hundreds of *critical / critically* endangered species.

e Our company cars are fuelled by renewable solar-*powering / powered* energy.

3 Complete the text below with phrases from the box.

As a result   For example   For instance
Furthermore   In summary

Renewable energy is energy produced from natural sources that replenish themselves. Sunlight and wind, ...[1], are sources that are constantly being replenished. The benefits are obvious. There are no harmful carbon emissions. ....[2], there is no air or water pollution. Coal power stations, ...[3], emit mercury, lead, sulphur dioxide and dangerous metals into the atmosphere. ....[4], the ground and water supply becomes contaminated. ....[5], renewable energy has the potential to provide all our energy needs without harming our planet.

Reading

4 Read the information about sustainable degree courses, then answer the questions that follow.

> **Sustainability degree courses**
>
> Are you passionate about the environment? Do you want to help protect our planet for future generations? Then why not consider a degree in sustainability studies? Our interdisciplinary programme combines social and environmental sciences with ecological and business studies. You'll learn to develop innovative solutions to the challenges posed by climate change and environmental damage. You will build skills across a range of industries, including corporate, non-profit and governmental sectors. This course of study can help you become a well-rounded candidate for an environmental or conservation role in the green industry. We'll help you to achieve your career goals to make a significant contribution to solving the climate crisis.

a Who is this the intended audience for this text?

....

b What type of background knowledge do you think would be needed for this course?

....

c Suggest two examples of jobs that this course would qualify someone for.

....

d Which words in the text match these meanings?

   i   enthusiastic   ....

   ii   multi-subject   ....

   iii   blend   ....

   iv   original   ....

   v   develop   ....

   vi   variety   ....

   vii   exceptional   ....

e Would you be interested in this degree course? Why, or why not?

....

Writing

5 Choose one of the tasks below and write a plan for an expository essay in your notebook. Then write an essay of about 250 words.

> Compare and contrast the use of fossil fuels and renewable alternative energy sources.

> Explain how the use of fossil fuels has contributed to climate change and why it is important to reduce our carbon footprint.

> Describe three ways in which we could take action in our daily lives to help reduce carbon dioxide emissions.

REFLECTION

Write answers to these questions in your notebook.

a How has your understanding of sustainability changed after studying this unit? Write your own definition of sustainability.

b Look back at the new words you learnt in this unit. What strategies did you use to remember their meanings?

c What are five criteria you would use to evaluate how sustainable your school or home is?

d Look at your last essay and find three places where you could add linking words or phrases.

e What have you found to be the best way to gather ideas for an expository essay? How could you improve this technique?

9 Fabric and fashion

Think about it: Ancient textiles and clothing

A	B	C
....	....	_wooden_
wool	_silk_	....
....	....	....

D	E	F
cotton	....	_dyed_
....	_leather_	....
....	....	....

1   Choose one word from each box to create a description of each of the pictures. Use each word only once.

~~cotton~~	indigo	fabric
~~dyed~~	~~leather~~	loom
knitted	~~silk~~	machine
stitched	spinning	shoes
~~wooden~~	weaving	socks
woven	~~wool~~	textiles

2 Complete the description with words from the box.
There are two words you do not need to use.

| articles | clothing | dyed | fabric | garments | indigo |
| leather | linen | sewn | woven |

Fashion in Ancient Assyria

The Assyrian Empire existed from 900 to 600 BCE, in the region between the Tigris and Euphrates Rivers that is now Iraq, Turkey and Syria. This picture shows the costume of an Assyrian king. Assyrian dress consisted of two basic ....[1] of clothing, a shawl and a tunic. These could vary in length and in style. The most common ....[2] for clothing was wool, although ....[3] was also used for better quality ....[4] and was ....[5] in various bright colours, including red, green, yellow, purple and ....[6]. The picture shows a king wearing an ankle-length tunic with short sleeves and a long shawl draped over one shoulder. The tunic and shawl are both richly patterned, and there is a heavy fringe on the hem of the shawl. The length and style of these garments indicate his high status. His sandals are ....[7] from leather and he wears a pointed hat ....[8] with bands of gold. The headwear and the heavy bracelets on his wrists and arm are an additional sign of his elevated rank.

Costume of an Assyrian king

3 Find words in the description that match these meanings.

a   a type of jewellery   ....

b   a large piece of cloth like a cloak   ....

c   the bottom edge of a garment   ....

d   folded or wrapped   ....

e   a decorative edge of strips or threads   ....

Challenge

4 Choose one of these ancient civilisations and find out about their clothing. Write a short description in your notebook. Use the description in Exercise 2 as a model.

- Ancient Egypt
- Ancient Rome
- the Aztec Empire
- the Ottoman Empire

Cultural studies: The link between culture and fashion

1 **You are going to read an article about silk. Before you read, answer these questions to find out what you already know about this material.**

   a   What is silk made from?

   ....

   b   When was silk first made?

   ....

   c   Which countries are the main silk producers?

   ....

2 **Read the article and find out if your answers were correct.**

The history of silk

1 Silk is one of the most luxurious fabrics in the world. It is soft yet strong and is used in many of the finest garments, as well as for detailed decoration techniques such as embroidery and appliqué.

2 Silk production – known as sericulture – originated in China in the 4th century BCE. The fabric was highly valued, which led to the development of a vast trading network across Asia and into Europe known as the Silk Road. The secrets of silk manufacture were closely guarded in China, and the country maintained a monopoly on its production for 2000 years.

3 Around 300 CE, silk cultivation reached Japan, and afterwards spread to Turkey and Mesopotamia, and eventually to Europe. By the 16th century, both France and Italy had a successful silk trade, especially after the introduction of the spinning wheel helped to accelerate the manufacturing process.

4 The discovery of silk manufacture is **attributed** to a Chinese princess, Xi Lingshi, thanks to a silkworm cocoon that dropped into her tea while she was sitting under a mulberry tree. She realised that the soaked cocoon could be unravelled into a fine thread.

5 The large-scale production of silk is time-consuming and labour-intensive. First, the silkworm eggs are **incubated** at a temperature of 18 °C, increasing to 25 °C. Once the worms have **hatched**, they feed on mulberry leaves until they are large enough to spin a **cocoon**. After about nine days, the cocoons are dipped in hot water and the thread is unwound. Each cocoon produces about 900 metres of a single thread.

6 Silk is considered to be both environmentally and economically sustainable. Its manufacture maintains tree cover and the fabric is 100% **decomposable**. It provides economic income for thousands of workers in China, India and other countries. However, there is some debate around its ethical viability in relation to animal cruelty. As a result, alternatives to silk, derived from plant-based sources such as bamboo or citrus by-products, are currently under development.

A man from Thailand creating traditional ethnic silk fabric

9 Fabric and fashion

> **attribute:** to say or think that something is the result of a particular thing
>
> **incubate:** when eggs are kept warm so the creature inside can develop
>
> **hatch:** to break out of an egg
>
> **cocoon:** a cover that protect some animals while they are developing into adults
>
> **decomposable:** can be broken down into compost
>
> **by-product:** something made as result of making something else

3   Which of the following information is included in the article?
    Match them with the correct paragraph number. Two items are not used.

   a   how silk is made ☐   e   how silk production became global ☐
   b   why silk is good for your skin ☐   f   how much it costs to produce silk ☐
   c   how silk was invented ☐   g   whether silk harms the environment ☐
   d   where silk was first made ☐   h   why silk is highly valued ☐

4   Answer these questions.

   a   Why do you think the manufacture of silk was kept secret for so long?
       ....
   b   Why do you think silk is considered a luxury fabric?
       ....
   c   Why do some people consider silk production to be controversial?
       ....

5   Find these words in the article. Explain what each one means in your own words.

   a   closely guarded   ....
   b   accelerate   ....
   c   unravelled   ....
   d   labour-intensive ....
   e   ethical   ....

6   Draw a flowchart in your notebook to illustrate six steps in the process
    of silk manufacture.

Challenge

7   Find out about the manufacture of one of these textiles.
    Write a paragraph in your notebook.

   linen   cotton   wool

107

Use of English: Negative and positive quantifiers

USE OF ENGLISH

Ethical fashion sounds good, but not everyone can agree on its definition. For some people, it means that there is no leather or fur. For others, it means that all the workers are treated fairly. Sustainability is important too; not all items of clothing are equally easy to recycle, for example. Not every consumer thinks about ethical fashion when they are shopping, but the benefits of choosing clothes that have little or no negative impact on the environment is something that none of us would disagree with.

Check!

1 Read the description above. Underline the phrases that use the words *every, all, not, no* or *none*.

2 Complete the rules with one or more of these words: *every, all, no, none*.

    a   We can use .... or .... to form indefinite pronouns.

    b   We can use .... or .... with countable nouns.

    c   We can use .... or .... with plural and uncountable nouns.

    d   We can use .... or .... + *of* before articles, nouns, demonstratives (*this, that*), possessives (*my, your*) and pronouns (*us, you, them*).

Notice

3 What type of verb is used with *all* and *every*? How is the meaning different?

....

....

Focus

4 **Circle the correct words to complete the sentences.**

    a   Not *everyone / anyone* is interested in ethical fashion.

    b   Not *all / every* people have the same taste in clothing.

    c   *No / None* of our fabrics uses toxic dyes.

    d   *Every / All* of our designs use vegetarian materials.

    e   Not *every / all* clothing we throw away is recyclable.

Practice

5 Correct the mistake in each of these sentences.

a All the information cannot be found online.

b Not every fashion brand isn't committed to ethical fashion.

c None our dress designs use synthetic fabrics.

d Every clothing manufacturer doesn't use eco-certified cotton.

e Not every of our textiles is organically produced.

> **GET IT RIGHT!**
>
> It is not common to use *all/every* + noun followed by a negative verb.
>
> Example:
> *Not all people like the same fashion.* (not *All people don't like*)

Challenge

6 Complete the text using words from the box.

all (x3)   every (x2)   everyone   no   none   not   nothing

Join the ethical fashion revolution! ....¹ of us here at Eco-friendly Fashion are committed to reducing the negative impact of the fashion industry. Not ....² knows that the fashion industry is one of the biggest global contributors to pollution. On our website, you will find ....³ made from polyester or acrylic. Instead, ...⁴ our clothes are made from organic cotton and linen. ....⁵ item of clothing is certified as having been produced using fair and sustainable practices. And ....⁶ of our fabric is wasted – ....⁷ unused scrap is recycled or composted. But ....⁸ all our ideas are about clothing. We've thought about our packaging as well. There's absolutely ....⁹ plastic; ....¹⁰ our packaging is made from 100% recycled paper.

Use of English: Linking words to show contrast

USE OF ENGLISH

Following fashion trends

Following fashion trends can be a fun way to keep up with your friends. Nevertheless, the pressure can be stressful. Whereas in the past, people bought new outfits just two or three times a year, they now change their fashion styles almost weekly. On the one hand, it is easy to understand why wearing up-to-date clothes is important. On the other hand, it might discourage you from finding your own unique clothing style.

Check!

1 Read the article above. Underline the linking words and phrases.

Notice

2 Which linking word in the article can be used to join two clauses? ....

Focus

3 Match the two parts of the sentences.

a On the one hand, fashion generates a lot of jobs. On the other hand,

b Whereas online fashion photos may look trendy and cute,

c Many cheap fashion items are made of synthetic materials,

d Natural fabrics are generally more expensive. Nevertheless,

e Buying new clothes every week might seem like fun. However,

i they waste a lot of resources when they end up in the landfill.

ii many garment workers are overworked and underpaid.

iii they can trap you into buying clothes you don't really need.

iv they don't fall to pieces after washing and usually last a long time.

v while longer lasting products are generally more expensive.

Practice

4 **Correct the mistake in each of these sentences.**

a Buying new clothes is fun, however, some people can't afford it.

b In the one hand, not everyone enjoys posting pictures on social media.

c Expressing yourself through fashion is enjoyable. Whereas, some find it stressful.

d While developing your identity is important. Fashion isn't the only way to do this.

e Following fashion trends is a popular hobby. There are nevertheless other hobbies that are just as fun.

Challenge

5 **Read these pros and cons of buying fashion online. Write five sentences using them and linking words from this unit.**

Pros:
- Clothing is cheaper.
- You can buy things faster.
- You can keep up with fashion trends.
- It is more convenient.
- You can compare process at different stores.

Cons:
- You can spend more money than you can afford.
- You can't try the clothing on.
- It is sometimes different or the wrong size.
- You often have to pay delivery costs.
- Some websites sell personal information.

....

....

....

....

....

....

....

....

> **GET IT RIGHT!**
>
> *Nevertheless* and *however* are frequently used at the start of a sentence and are followed by a comma. They can also be used mid-sentence. In that case, there is a comma on either side.
>
> Example:
> *Fast fashion is often associated with more consumer choice. The cost to the environment,* **however,** *is considerable.*

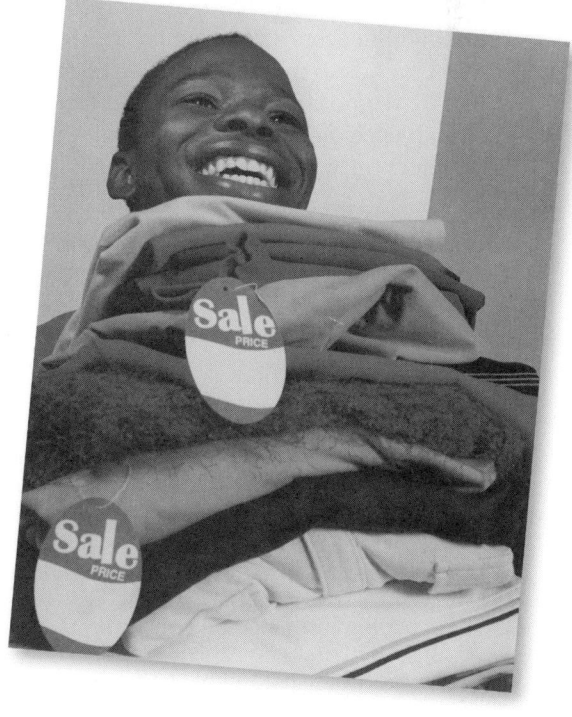

Academic writing: Advantages and disadvantages essay

1 Look at the picture. What do you think this person is doing? Write one idea.

....

....

....

....

2 Read the task notes a–l for an essay about fashion influencers. Decide which paragraph each belongs with. Write the correct letter: A, B, C or D.

Fashion influencers are a popular way for fashion brands to market their latest products. What are the positive and negative effects of their influence on consumers? Do you think the advantages outweigh the disadvantages?

- **A** Introduction
- **B** Advantages paragraph
- **C** Disadvantages paragraph
- **D** Conclusion

- a has a large following on social media
- b can promote unhealthy or unsustainable fashion choices
- c need to develop your own criteria for what you buy
- d followers can lose their individuality and feel pressure to conform
- e have a big influence on consumer fashion choices
- f can promote sustainable and ethical fashion choices
- g keep a sense of your own individual personal style
- h makes fashion accessible to more people
- i persuades people to buy products via social media posts
- j should be critical of the values behind a fashion influencer's blog
- k saves time searching for products you like
- l can post misleading information in order to promote their sponsors

> **WRITING TIP**
>
> An advantages and disadvantages essay asks you to present the positive and negative sides of a given topic. You will need to include reasons and examples to support your arguments. You may be asked to express your opinion.

3 Complete these sentences with linking words that show contrast.

a .... many fashion influencers aim to help their followers, some of them are paid to promote certain brands.

b It is easy to be convinced that you need to buy a new T-shirt.

.............................., it is worth taking a moment to consider whether it is really necessary.

c Fashion influencers can keep us up to date. On ...., they can encourage us to buy things we can't really afford.

4 Write an essay in your notebook to answer the essay question in Exercise 2. Write 200–250 words.

5 Read your essay aloud. Find ways to improve it by using linking words and phrases.

Check your progress

Vocabulary

1 Complete the description with words from the box.

clothing	dyed	embroidered
fabric	garment	knitted	sewn
textile	weaving	woven

Traditional Andean clothing

Andean ....¹ traditions date back to before the Aztec and Incan empires, and include a wide variety of ....² and dying techniques. Traditional Andean ....³ is typically made from alpaca or llama wool that is ....⁴ on a hand loom and ....⁵ bright colours. Men often wear a cap ....⁶ from alpaca or llama wool. Known as a *chullo*, it has flaps to keep the ears warm and can be tied under the chin. Another traditional ....⁷ is the *poncho*, which is a large piece of ....⁸ with a hole in the middle for the head to pass through. Women often wear brightly coloured jackets and wide skirts. Bands of ribbon are ....⁹ onto the skirt to indicate the wearer's village or region. They also wear a small cape or cloak that is ....¹⁰ with brightly coloured geometric designs, animals and flowers.

Grammar

2 In your notebook, rewrite the sentences using the words provided.

a Some people don't think that using leather in fashion is ethical. (everyone)

b Some employees disagree with having a dress code at work. (all)

c All our products are made from natural fibres. (every)

d Every dress is handmade by local artisans. (none, machine-made)

3 Circle the correct words to complete the text.

Which is better, linen or cotton?

*Although / Because*¹ both are made from natural plant fibres, linen and cotton are two very different textiles. Linen is made from the stems of flax plants. Cotton, *on the one hand / however*², comes from plants that produce small fibre-filled seed pods. Flax plants are grown in France, Belgium and Italy, which have cooler climates, *however / while*³ cotton is grown in the warmer climate zones of China, India, Brazil and Turkey. Flax needs almost no irrigation or fertilisation. Cotton, *on the other hand / whereas*⁴, uses large quantities of water, pesticides and fertilisers. *As a result / Furthermore*⁵, linen is an extremely sustainable crop. Linen is a little more expensive than cotton. *Consequently / Nevertheless*⁶, its high level of sustainability and durability makes it an excellent choice of fabric for every season.

9 Fabric and fashion

Reading

4 Read the paragraph below. Find synonyms or explain the meaning of the words (a–e).

> **Upcycled clothing**
>
> The latest trend in fashion has nothing to do with the glamorous catwalks of Paris or New York. The biggest fashion trend this year is upcycling. Upcycled fashion involves creating new garments out of old or unused clothing and textiles. Using up scraps or end-of-line fabric that are usually wasted is an innovative way to reduce the fashion industry's negative impact on the environment. Upcycling increases the value of existing clothing by cutting and restyling garments into unique ready-to-wear pieces. So why not join the upcycling revolution? It's the future of fashion for our planet.

a glamorous

....

b scraps

....

c end-of-line

....

d innovative

....

e unique

....

5 Answer these questions about the article in Exercise 4.

a What is the purpose of this text?

....

....

b How is upcycling different from recycling?

....

....

c Give two reasons why upcycling is good for the environment.

....

....

d Would you be interested in upcycled clothing? Why or why not?

....

....

Writing

6 Choose one of these two tasks and make notes for an essay. Then write the essay in your notebook. Write 250–300 words.

Fast fashion is thought to expand consumer choices and make fashion more available to everyone. Do you think that the advantages of fast fashion outweigh the disadvantages?

Nowadays, many clothes are made from synthetic fabrics because they are cheaper. Do you think that the advantages of using these fabrics outweigh the disadvantages?

REFLECTION

Write answers to these questions in your notebook.

a How did this unit make you think differently about clothing and textiles? Do you think fashion is important? Why or why not?

b What are three goals you would have if you started your own fashion design company?

c What strategies for working out the meaning of new words did you use in this unit? Give two examples.

d Look at your last essay and find three places where you could use linking words to show contrast.

e What tips would you give a classmate for writing an advantages/disadvantages essay?

10 Fiction and the future

Think about it: Stories from the future

1 Read the descriptions of different science-fiction TV series. What do they all have in common?

....

> **We asked you to tell us about your favourite sci-fi TV series. Here are your top picks.**
>
> **A** The year is 2265. A starship and its crew are on a peaceful mission to explore space. While navigating the solar system, they discover new worlds and civilisations. Their spacecraft is equipped with new inventions such as teleporters that beam them down onto other planets and universal translators that allow them to communicate in any language.
>
> **B** After a virus wipes out most of the human population, two teenagers emerge from an underground safety shelter where they have been living for the past five years. They discover that civilisation as they knew it has disappeared and they set out to search for other survivors so they can start to rebuild their lives.
>
> **C** A young woman is taking part in a new virtual reality game. She finds out that the simulation she has entered is actually in the future and that she is travelling between parallel worlds. In the future world, she encounters intelligent robots that can control humans and she realises the game is more dangerous than she thought.
>
> **D** Earth has been destroyed by a nuclear disaster and the only survivors are on an international space station orbiting Earth. Running out of resources, they decide to send a team of young people back to the planet surface to find out whether it is safe to live there or not.

2 Write the letter(s) of the TV series in Exercise 1 next to the correct description.
   Which TV series…

   a portrays life on Earth after a catastrophe? ....
   b depicts futuristic technology? ....
   c mentions technology we have today? ....
   d describes people with hope for the future? ....
   e is about time travel? ....
   f imagines an uninhabitable Earth? ....

3 Read the plot summary of a science-fiction novel. Would you like to read this book? Why or why not?

   ....

Red Mars by Kim Stanley Robinson

The first volume in this epic scientific trilogy by the award-winning author Kim Stanley Robinson is an ambitious narrative chronicling the colonisation of Mars. For centuries, humans have been fascinated by the challenge of its hostile climate and forbidding landscape. Finally, a group of colonists is about to land on Mars. Their goal is to transform Mars into a habitable planet for humans. Using giant satellite mirrors to reflect light and drilling vast tunnels kilometres beneath the surface, they discover how much is required of them to change the planet before the planet changes them.

4 Read these statements about the plot summary above and circle true (T), false (F) or not given (NG).

   a There are three more books in this series. T F NG
   b The story combines speculative fiction and science. T F NG
   c The goal of this mission is to build a home on Mars. T F NG
   d The colonists have escaped Earth because it is uninhabitable. T F NG
   e Conditions on Mars are compatible with supporting human life. T F NG
   f The task of the colonists is likely to be dangerous and difficult. T F NG

Challenge

5 Choose a science-fiction TV series or book that you have enjoyed. In your notebook, write a short summary using about 100 words. Use the descriptions in Exercises 1 and 3 as a model.

Literature: Science fiction

1. What is science fiction? Write a definition in your own words.

   ....

2. Read the article. Is your definition the same?

Science fiction: A beginner's guide

Have you ever wondered what it would be like to go to the moon? Or travel forward in time? Then science fiction is definitely for you! Not sure where to start? Read on to get some ideas about how to begin your sci-fi reading adventure.

What is science fiction?

Science fiction – or sci-fi – is a genre of speculative fiction that deals with possible future worlds. According to author Isaac Asimov, 'Science fiction can be defined as that branch of literature which deals with the reaction of human beings to changes in science and technology'. Some of its many subgenres include themes of space exploration, parallel universes, time travel and artificial intelligence. As well as exploring the consequences of advances in technology and science, science fiction can also be socially reflective, providing a commentary on contemporary social issues.

What are different categories within science fiction?

Some science fiction focuses on the more technical and scientific aspects of the future. Sometimes known as hard sci-fi, it includes detailed descriptions involving physics, astronomy, computer science, chemistry and biology. Even if it describes technology that hasn't been invented yet, it is based on developments that are theoretically possible. Examples of this subgenre include *2001: A Space Odyssey* by Arthur C. Clarke and *I, Robot* by Isaac Asimov.

Another category of science fiction, sometimes known as soft sci-fi, while also focused on futuristic aspects of technology, is more concerned with the social implications of technology and includes details relating to psychology, sociology, politics and anthropology. Scientific developments can be based on technology that hasn't yet been proven or developed. More attention is given to the characters and how they and society in general respond to the new technology. Examples of this subgenre include *Earthsea* by Ursula Le Guin and *Dune* by Frank Herbert.

Why is science fiction important?

Science fiction is important for several reasons. First, it's exciting and fun! It can take us on a fascinating adventure into an immersive alternate reality. Not only that, it can also help us to see our own world differently and try to understand our society and ourselves better. Finally, science fiction can predict possible ways in which our world may change and can either warn us or encourage us with hope for the future.

3 Answer these questions.

a Who is the intended audience for this article?

....

b What are the main similarities between soft and hard sci-fi?

....

c What are the main differences between soft and hard sci-fi?

....

d Which type of sci-fi would you recommend to a newcomer to this genre and why?

....

e Which type of sci-fi would you be most interested in and why?

....

Challenge

4 **Think of a science-fiction novel or film. How closely does it resemble the descriptions in this article? Write a brief explanation.**

....

....

....

....

....

....

Use of English: *it* and *there*

USE OF ENGLISH

Fact or fiction?

It is generally agreed that science fiction explores the possible impact of scientific advances. It could be argued, however, that the reverse is also true; science fiction may inspire the development of new technologies. Although intelligent robots have long been dreamt of as a scientific goal, it is equally possible that human-computer interaction imagined in science fiction has influenced theoretical research design. It would be difficult to evaluate the precise influence of fiction on scientific research, but it is certainly undeniable that the AI of today bears an uncanny similarity to the talking computers in films and books of more than 50 years ago.

Check!

1 Read the paragraph above. Underline phrases that use it as a dummy subject.

2 Match the examples you underlined with the descriptions below.

   a   *it* + passive + a clause.   ....

   b   *it* + *be* + adjective + infinitive   ....

   c   *it* + *be* + adjective + a clause   ....

Notice

3 Which of the underlined phrases express certainty? Which ones are less certain?

....

....

Focus

4 **Rewrite these sentences using *it* as a subject.**

   a   People sometimes think that science fiction can predict the future.

       ....

   b   Reading science fiction that depicts a dark future for our planet can be depressing.

       ....

c The fact that many inventions were first thought of by sci-fi writers is amazing.

   ....

d Sci-fi video games seem to be getting more popular with teenagers.

   ....

Practice

5 Complete these sentences using *it* or *there* + *be*.

a .... some disagreement about how many galaxies there are in the universe.

b .... widely predicted that robots will take over many of our jobs.

c .... many reasons why science fiction is so popular.

d .... difficult to predict whether solar-powered cars will become commonplace.

Challenge

6 Complete the description with phrases from the box.

| it has been   it is impossible   it is possible   it is   it seems likely |
| it will be   there are   there is   there will be |

LANGUAGE TIP

We use *there is/are* to introduce a new subject (a noun or noun phrase). We use *it is/was* to introduce (or anticipate) a complex subject that comes later in the sentence.

Examples:
There is a lot of speculation about the use of artificial intelligence.

It is likely that every home will have its own robot in ten years' time.

What will the future look like?

....¹ many ways in which advances in technology will change our future.

....² suggested, for example, that AI will become highly sophisticated.

....³ that robots will take over many of our jobs. Secondly, ...⁴ that we will have machines at home that diagnose and treat illnesses. Thirdly, ...⁵ predicted that instead of going to school, students will attend virtual classrooms. Finally, ...⁶ to be absolutely sure, but ....⁷ little doubt that transportation will change. ....⁸ unusual to see individual cars and ....⁹ more driverless vehicles as well as flying taxis.

Use of English: Hedging language

USE OF ENGLISH

Life on Mars

The possibility of life on Mars tends to be a popular theme in science fiction. There seems to be some evidence to suggest that there may have been water on the planet's surface between three and four billion years ago. It appears that life might possibly have existed under those conditions, but this does not necessarily indicate that this was definitely the case. It is believed that future research expeditions to Mars could potentially support or disprove this theory.

Check!

1 Read the description above.
   Underline examples of hedging language.

Notice

2 Match words from the hedging language you identified with these descriptions.

   a hedging verbs   ....
   b reporting verbs   ....
   c modal verbs   ....
   d adverbs of uncertainty ....
   e *it* as a subject   ....

Focus

3 Complete these sentences with words from the box.

   | There may not | It could be | There appears | It seems that | It would seem |

   a .... argued that we should search for other planets to live on.
   b .... be any life forms, even on habitable planets.
   c .... colonies in space may be possible in the future.

d .... to be some evidence of water on Mars.

e .... to indicate that life on other planets might be possible.

Practice

4 Rewrite these sentences using the words provided in brackets.

a Space research will find evidence of life on other planets. (widely, believe, may)

It ....

b Space travel will become commonplace in the next decade. (appear, could)

It ....

c Habitable conditions existed on Mars a long time ago. (there, might)

There ....

d Humans will build colonies on Mars in the future. (seem, possibility, may)

There ....

e Humans will live on satellites orbiting Earth. (seem, possible, might)

It ....

Challenge

5 Write five ways in which space research and technology may develop in the future. Make brief notes in the box. Then rewrite your notes using hedging language from this lesson.

Notes
....
....
....

....
....
....
....
....

LANGUAGE TIP

Hedging language refers to the way in which a writer expresses caution or uncertainty. It is a way of softening language to make claims less absolute. Hedging language includes verbs such as *seem and appear*, which can be used with *it* or *there*.

Examples:
There seems/appears to be a tendency for science fiction to warn us about disasters.

It appears/seems that many sci-fi writers have been able to predict future inventions.

Academic writing: Critical analysis – fiction

1 Read the title and book summary.
  Write three questions you would like to ask about the story.

> **The City of Ember**
>
> The city of Ember was built as a last refuge for the human race. Two hundred years later, the great lamps that light the city are beginning to dim.

....

....

....

2 Read the opening paragraphs of *The City of Ember* by Jeanne DuPrau.
  What do you think the title of the chapter means?

Chapter 1

Assignment Day

In the city of Ember, the sky was always dark. The only light came from great flood lamps mounted on the buildings and at the tops of poles in the middle of the larger squares. When the lights were on, they cast a yellowish glow over the streets; people walking by threw long shadows that shortened and then stretched out again. When the lights were off, as they were between nine at night and six in the morning, the city was so dark that people might as well have been wearing blindfolds.

Sometimes darkness fell in the middle of the day. The city of Ember was old, and everything in it, including the power lines, was in need of repair. So now and then the lights would flicker and go out. These were terrible moments for the people of Ember. As they came to a halt in the middle of the street or stood stock-still in their houses, afraid to move in the utter blackness, they were reminded of something they preferred not to think about:

that someday the lights of the city might go out and never come back on.

But most of the time life proceeded as it always had. Grown people did their work, and younger people, until they reached the age of twelve, went to school. On the last day of their final year, which was called Assignment Day, they were given jobs to do.

10 Fiction and the future

3 Answer these questions.

a   What adjectives would you use to describe the atmosphere in this opening to the story?

....

b   List all words connected with light or dark. What is the effect of these words?

....

....

c   How does the writer make you curious about the story? What do you want to know more about? Write three ideas.

....

....

....

d   Choose one visual image mentioned in the extract and describe its effect.

....

e   How does the final paragraph contrast with the rest of the extract?

....

f   What is surprising about the final line?

....

4 Use your answers to Exercise 3 to write a short critical review (about 150 words) of the extract in your notebook.

> **WRITING TIP**
>
> A critical analysis of a piece of literature considers the writer's technique and how they use this to convey specific ideas. It is important to think about how the author uses character, tone, setting and imagery to achieve certain effects. Unlike a book review, a critical analysis does not need to include your own opinion or a summary of the story.

Check your progress

Vocabulary

1 **Answer these questions in your own words.**

   a Why is reading literature a form of escapism?

      ....
      ....

   b In what ways can science fiction be socially reflective?

      ....
      ....

   c What does cognitive estrangement in literature make the reader do?

      ....
      ....

   d What is teleportation an example of?

      ....
      ....

Grammar

2 **In your notebook, rewrite these sentences using the words provided in brackets.**

   a Science fiction speculates about the future. (it, generally, agree)

   b Sci-fi novels often describe Earth after a catastrophe. (seem, tend)

   c Some people have said that sci-fi should focus on more optimistic views of the future. (it, suggest, perhaps)

   d Some elements of science fiction will become scientific facts. (there, evidence, indicate, may, possibly)

   e Humans will be able to live on Mars one day. (appear, potentially, could)

10 Fiction and the future

Reading

3 Read the paragraph and then answer the questions.

What is 'futures studies' and how can it help us improve our world?

Futures studies, or futures research, is the systematic study of possible, probable and preferable futures. The field has broadened into an exploration of alternative futures and deepened to investigate the worldviews and mythologies that underlie our collective prospects.

Governments and leaders around the world are increasingly looking to systemic foresight to manage uncertainty and build resilience. For example, the government of the United Arab Emirates has a Ministry for the Future, and the UN Secretary General recently proposed a global Summit of the Future.

Futurists collaborate with businesses, governments and other partners to explore future scenarios and help people think about – and prepare for – things that haven't happened yet.

a What is the purpose of this text?

....

b Why is the word 'futures' used instead of 'future'?

....

c How have futures studies changed in recent years?

....

d How can futurists help improve our world? Give two examples.

....

e Would you be interested in studying this field of research? Why or why not?

....

Writing

4 Choose one novel that you have read recently and write a critical analysis in your notebook. Write 300–350 words.

REFLECTION

Write answers to these questions in your notebook.

a How has your view of the future changed after studying this unit?
b How do you think science fiction helps us to think about the future?
c What is one book mentioned in this unit that you would like to read? Why?
d Why is it important to use hedging language in your essays?
e What are the main challenges of writing a critical analysis of a piece of literature?

Key phrases bank

Unit 1

Adverbs for expressing attitude
clearly
fortunately
honestly
hopefully
sadly
surprisingly
unfortunately

Functional language for discussions
Carry on…
Don't stop there…
From my point of view…
Go on…
How about you…?
I feel we should…
I know just how you feel.
I'm with you…
The way I see it…
What about you…?
What do you reckon…?
What makes you say that?

Signalling relationships between ideas
for instance
furthermore
in other words
like
moreover
such as
that is to say
to put it another way
what's more

Unit 2

Signposting
Additionally,…
And finally,…
Another (strategy) is to…
Equally,…
First of all,…
Firstly,…
Furthermore,…
However,…
I'm going to begin by…
In contrast,…
Next,…
On the other hand,…
Secondly,…
To explain more about that,…

Softening criticism
I can see that…
I can see what you're saying, but…
I just felt that…
I thought that…
I'd probably say…
I'm not sure…
It sounded as though…
It sounds good, but…
That could work, I agree, although…

Describing data
closely followed by
considerable variation
for the majority
the greatest proportion
the heaviest emphasis
the largest amount
the lowest/highest scoring
the trend for
this figure falls to

Unit 3

Impersonal language
Action is recommended in these areas…
Improvements can be made by…
The installation of…
The introduction of…
This proposal will…

Formal conditional structures
Should… decide to… it would…
Were… to… this would…

Key phrases bank

Unit 4

Signposting non-specific references
Research also shows…
There is general consensus…
There is strong evidence…

Agreeing
I know.
Sure. I'm with you on that.
That is so true.
True. But I'd go even further.
Yes. Very clever.

Debating language
A significant claim…
I refute your argument…
Opponents suggested…
Supporters claim…
The counter-claim is…
Those who rebut the claim…

Unit 5

Agreeing
Couldn't agree more.
I totally agree.
I'm with you on that.
That's just what I was thinking.

Disagreeing
I can see where you're coming from, however…
I take your point, but…
That's a good point, but I don't think I can agree with you.
You may be right, but I still think that…

Justifying opinions
I think… It means…
You make a good point, but I'm just wondering if…

Cohesive devices
furthermore
however
moreover
nevertheless
therefore

Unit 6

Speculating and making deductions
I suppose…
He might…
She may…
they could…
That can't be the reason.
Could it be…
There must…
It's possible…
Maybe it's…
Perhaps the…

Unit 7

Expressing certainty, manner and degree
… completely different…
… considerably improved…
… deliberately chose…
… regularly measured…
… significantly higher…
… undoubtedly show…

Unit 8

Fixed expressions
All in all…
All things considered…
At the end of the day…
Come to think of it…
When it comes down to it…
When you think about it…

Engaging and supporting others
I didn't know that…
So, am I right in saying that…
So, you're saying…
That isn't something I'd thought of…
That's really interesting…

Unit 9

Discourse functions

> But surely…
> I have to admit…
> I have to admit, I hadn't…
> I know this may not be a popular point of view…
> I see what you mean, but…
> It is true that…
> That may be true, but…
> We shouldn't lose sight of the fact that…

Linking words to show contrast

> … however…
> … nevertheless…
> … nonetheless…
> one the one hand… on the other hand…
> … whereas…
> … while…

Unit 10

Keeping the conversation flowing

> Absolutely. Couldn't agree more.
> Couldn't have said it better myself.
> I have a feeling that…
> I may be wrong but…
> I really think that…
> I'm not an expert, but…
> I'm pretty sure… I mean, look at…
> Sure. I think it's a great…
> That's an amazing idea.
> What are you trying to say?
> You can say that again!

Showing caution through hedging language

> It could be argued…
> It is generally agreed…
> It seems equally possible…
> It would be hard, if not impossible…

Irregular verb table

Infinitive	Past simple	Past participle
be	was, were	been
begin	began	begun
break	broke	broken
bring	brought	brought
buy	bought	bought
build	built	built
choose	chose	chosen
come	came	come
cost	cost	cost
cut	cut	cut
do	did	done
draw	drew	drawn
drive	drove	driven
eat	ate	eaten
feel	felt	felt
find	found	found
fly	flew	flown
get	got	got
give	gave	given
go	went	gone
have	had	had
hold	held	held
hurt	hurt	hurt
keep	kept	kept
know	knew	known
leave	left	left
lead	led	led
let	let	let
lie	lay	lain
lose	lost	lost
make	made	made
mean	meant	meant
meet	met	met
pay	paid	paid
put	put	put
run	ran	run

Infinitive	Past simple	Past participle
say	said	said
see	saw	seen
sell	sold	sold
send	sent	sent
set	set	set
sit	sat	sat
speak	spoke	spoken
spend	spent	spent
stand	stood	stood
take	took	taken
teach	taught	taught
tell	told	told
think	thought	thought
understand	understood	understood
wear	wore	worn
win	won	won
write	wrote	written

Acknowledgements

The authors and publishers acknowledge the following sources of copyright material and are grateful for the permissions granted. While every effort has been made, it has not always been possible to identify the sources of all the material used, or to trace all copyright holders. If any omissions are brought to our notice, we will be happy to include the appropriate acknowledgements on reprinting.

We would like to thank the following reviewers for providing feedback on the draft manuscript: Wenlian Yang and Mosharraf Hossain.

Unit 1 Text abridged from 'Young people who frequently argue with their parents are better citizens, research finds' from Cardiff University, reproduced with permission of the Licensor through PLSclear; **Unit 2** Text abridged from 'Why failure is the key to flying high' by Matthew Syed in the Guardian, Copyright Guardian News & Media Ltd; Text abridged from 'Playing with dolls helps children talk about how others feel' by Hannah Devlin in the Guardian, Copyright Guardian News & Media Ltd.; Text abridged from 'The Importance of failure: why Olympians and A-level students all need to fail' by Marc Smith in the Guardian, Copyright Guardian News & Media Ltd.; **Unit 3** Text adapted from 'Why are insects attracted to lights?' by Debbie Hadley taken from www.thoughtco.com, Dotdash Meridith Publishing; Text abridged from 'The big idea; is it time to stop worrying about stress?' in the Guardian, Copyright Guardian News & Media Ltd.; Blurb of *Winter of Our Discontent* by Susan Maushart, Penguin Random House Australia; **Unit 4** Text adapted from 'Celebrating the symbol of the computer age' in the Guardian, Copyright Guardian News & Media Ltd.; Extract from Hughes, J. (2016). '10 visual literacy activities for language learning', ETpedia, published and reproduced with permission of Pavillion Publishing and Media; **Unit 5** Text adapted from 'Inside Japan's first robot-staffed hotel' in the Guardian, Copyright Guardian News & Media Ltd.; Text abridged from 'Scientists try to teach robot to laugh at the right time' in the Guardian, Copyright Guardian News & Media Ltd.; Text adapted from *How it Works* Issue 131 'Top Secret Spy Tech – Will AI Take Over the World?' by Efan Irvine, reproduced with the permission of Future Publishing Limited; **Unit 6** Text extract from 'How We Judge Personality from Faces Depends on Our Pre-Existing Beliefs About How Personality Work', used with the permission of New York University; **Unit 10** Excerpt(s) from *The City Of Ember: The First Book Of Ember* by Jeanne DuPrau, copyright © 2003 by Jeanne DuPrau. Used by permission of Random House Children's Books, a division of Penguin Random House LLC. All rights reserved and reprinted by permission of Penguin Books Limited; extract from 'What is 'futures studies' and how can it help us improve our world?', used with the permission of World Economic Forum.

Thanks to the following for permission to reproduce images:

Cover Achim Thomae/GI; *Inside* **Unit 1** Triloks/GI; Shapecharge/GI; Beemore/GI; Kate Green/Getty Images for BoF; Ken Chernus/GI; Renata Angerami/GI; David Zach/GI; Eva-Katalin/GI; Lane Oatey/GI; Kali9/GI; SDI Productions/GI; **Unit 2** Digital Vision/GI; Tony Ding/Icon Sportswire via GI; Martinedoucet/GI; SDI Productions/GI; Geir Pettersen/GI; Image Source/GI; Alistair Berg/GI; Caia Image/GI; AFP/GI; Mickey Adair/GI; Bettmann/GI; Westend61; **Unit 3** Pier/GI; Michael Maconachie/GI; Calvindexter/GI; Klaus Vedfelt/GI; Jasmin Merdan/GI; Somyot Techapuwapat/GI; Westend61/GI; Jasmin Merdan/GI; Jgareri/GI; Urbanglimpses/GI; Cako74/GI; **Unit 4** Succession Picasso/DACS, London; Anadolu Agency/GI; George Rinhart/GI; Gabor Goncz/GI; Azmanl/GI; Martin Zwick/GI; Henryk Sadura/GI; Westend61/GI; Michael Ochs Archives/GI; Jon Hicks/GI; Hans Georg Roth/GI; Abraham Gonzalez Fernandez/GI; **Unit 5** The Asahi Shimbun/GI; Trevor Williams/GI; Charly Triballeau/AFP via GI; Westend61/GI; Dowell/GI; Sergii Iaremenko/GI; Izusek/GI; Onurdongel/GI; damaerre/GI; Freder/GI; Vertigo3d/GI; **Unit 6** Maskot/GI; Pamelajoemcfarlane/GI; Luvo/GI; Iancu Cojocar/GI; Aska/GI; Rosmarie Wirz/GI; SDI Productions/GI; Peter Dazeley/GI; Willie B. Thomas/GI; Lisegagne/GI; Sturti/GI; Thomas Barwick/GI; Gmvozd/GI; **Unit 7** Choksawatdikorn/GI; Universal History Archive/GI; Martyn Large/GI; Alexandrumagurean/GI; Cinoby/GI; Wild Horizon/GI; R A Kearton/GI; Rosemary Calvert/GI; Microgen Images/GI; Krisanapong Detraphiphat/GI; Himagine/GI; **Unit 8** Holger Leue/GI; Goodboy Picture Company/GI; Witthaya Prasongsin/GI; Tom Werner/GI; Spiderstock/GI; Ratsanai/GI; Alistair Berg/GI; Jacobs Stock Photography Ltd/GI; Johner Images/GI; Raul Arboleda/GI; Artistgndphotography/GI; **Unit 9** Westend61/GI; Srinophan69/GI; Prapass Pulsub/GI; Masaotaira/GI; Djelics/GI; Jake Warga/GI; Isabel Pavia/GI; Duncan1890/GI; Skaman306/GI; Baobao Ou/GI; Ryan Mcvay/GI; Peter Dazeley/GI; Ankit Sah/GI; Digital Vision/GI; Xavier Lorenzo/GI; Alvaro Gonzalez/GI; James Strachan/GI; **Unit 10** Xuanyu Han/GI; Sciepro/GI; Ilbusca/GI; Gremlin/GI; Peter Cade/GI; Eoneren/GI; Mark Garlick/GI; Janiecbros/GI; Viaframe/GI; Gremlin/GI; Edwin Tan/GI; Pcess609/GI

Key: GI = Getty Images